The

CHICKS WITH STICKS®
GUIDE *to* CROCHET

The
CHICKS WITH STICKS®
GUIDE to CROCHET

learn to crochet
with more than 30 cool, easy patterns

NANCY QUEEN AND MARY ELLEN O'CONNELL

Watson-Guptill Publications / New York

First published in 2008 by Watson-Guptill Publications,
Nielsen Business Media, a division of The Nielsen Company
770 Broadway, New York, NY 10003
www.watsonguptill.com

Library of Congress Cataloging-in-Publication Data

Queen, Nancy.
  The Chicks with Sticks guide to crochet : learn to crochet with more than thirty cool,
easy patterns / by Nancy Queen and Mary Ellen O'Connell.
     p. cm.
  Includes bibliographical references and index.
  ISBN-13: 978-0-8230-0676-2 (pbk. : alk. paper)
  ISBN-10: 0-8230-0676-X (pbk. : alk. paper)
  1. Crocheting—Patterns. I. O'Connell, Mary Ellen. II. Title. III. Title: Guide to crochet.
  TT825.Q514 2008
  746.43'4—dc22
                              2007036432

Executive Editor Joy Aquilino
Development Editor Amy Vinchesi
Art Director Timothy Hsu
Production Director Alyn Evans

Printed in China

First printing, 2008

1 2 3 4 5 6 7 8 9 / 15 14 13 12 11 10 09 08 07

To Dan, Dave, and Hadley.

And special thanks to our husbands,

Chris & Ben, for their unwavering support

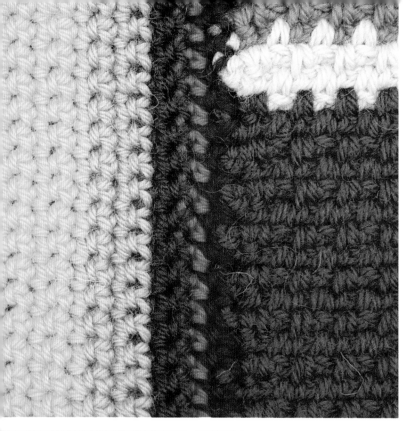

CONTENTS

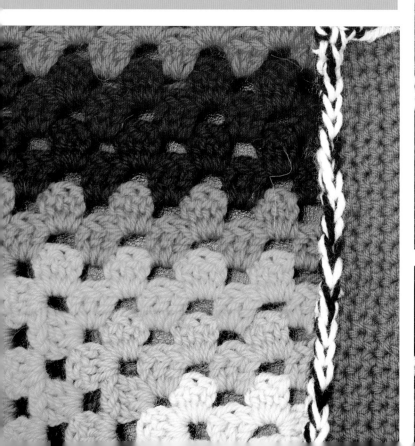

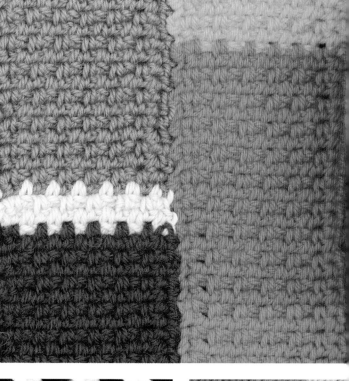

INTRODUCTION

Welcome to No Fear, No Sweat, No Problem Crocheting

This is our philosophy of learning to crochet in the fastest, easiest, and most effective way possible! You will learn to crochet a little bit at a time and will practice each technique with an interesting project. You won't feel overwhelmed with projects that are too complicated; instead you'll discover projects that keep your hands busy, your mind a little challenged, and your soul satisfied.

It's always a little intimidating when you try something new. We take the fear out of learning to crochet by providing you with terms and projects that are easy to master. Often we see beginners jump into projects that are too difficult; and they end up feeling overwhelmed and frustrated, and quit before they even start. You won't feel that way with this book!

You CAN Take It with You

Do you have a busy lifestyle, yet you are searching for something to spark your creativity? Do you want something to keep you occupied while your husband/significant other is relentlessly flipping channels on the TV, or while waiting for an appointment, or on your travel commute? Crochet fits the bill; plus it's a great way to relax and unwind. A recent Harvard study found that crochet has the same great Zen qualities as yoga (if only it could help us lose a few pounds as well!).

Crochet is portable, so you can take it anywhere: to a sporting event or doctor's office, on an airplane, even on a lunch break. We are "The Chicks with Sticks" because, quite frankly, you will never find us without our hooks and needles. We are addicted, and you will find us at the next Y.A. (Yarn-o-holics Anonymous) meeting proclaiming it proudly. Like you, we are busy gals, but we love

Sorry, No Crocheted Toilet Paper Cover Patterns in the Book!

You **WILL** find patterns that are timeless and sophisticated and that have an updated edge.

You **WON'T** find patterns that are so trendy, no one above the age of ten could wear them.

You **WON'T** find tedious projects with lots of charts and color changes or complex stitches.

You **WILL** find easy-to-follow step-by-step instructions to learn how to crochet.

You **WILL** find fun, relaxing projects that may have an interesting stitch repeat to keep you on your toes but are not so complex you can't take your eyes off them for a second.

You **WILL** find information to help you select the right yarn and tools to crochet.

You **WILL** find helpful hints and tricks not usually covered in an instruction book.

You **WILL** find ideas on how to put more crochet in your life.

You **WILL** find some fun stuff, such as your Crochet Horoscope.

How This Book Is Set Up

The Chicks with Sticks® Guide to Crochet is arranged in lessons to help you learn crocheting step-by-step, with each lesson providing building blocks for the next. The first lesson will familiarize you with crochet hooks, tools, and yarns as well as explain how to read patterns and yarn labels. The next few lessons introduce the five basic crochet stitches. Each new lesson ends with a project or two with which you can test out your new skills. As the lessons advance, you'll be introduced to

the chance to kick off our shoes, put up our feet, and get those fingers moving. We enjoy projects where we don't necessarily have to pay too much attention because we are also busy gabbing, or we don't want to miss who-did-what on the latest episode of our favorite TV shows. Most importantly, crocheting is something we love! It's easy to learn and a lot of fun to do. We want you to be able to enjoy it as much as we do; and, hopefully, someday you'll teach others how to crochet.

more complex stitches, changing colors, and felting, and eventually get to try your hand at sweaters. We'll teach you our secrets for getting the best crochet results, including how to measure for a garment that fits, how to select yarns, and our Chicks Shorthand for effortless garment shaping. We wrap up with tips and ideas for meeting other crocheters in your community, starting a crochet club, and even sharing your hobby through charitable crocheting. Bring your perseverance and enthusiasm and let's get started!

CHEEP TRICKS

The Chicks are all about shortcuts. We like to find the easiest, yet most effective way to do stuff. So we've added some of our favorite Cheep Tricks throughout the book to help you learn the ins and outs of crochet often not mentioned in a book or pattern.

CHICK FEED

With each pattern you'll find a little Chick Feed. These tidbits of info let you know why we created each design to accompany a lesson and which skills you will master.

FLY THE COOP!

At the end of a project you'll get a chance to Fly the Coop! The increased crochet confidence you will have after completing a lesson may give you the desire to "wing it," so we give you ideas for personalizing your project, such as easy ways to alter the pattern, add embellishment, or other yarn alternatives. This will help spark your creativity and allow endless possibilities for each project.

Yarn Ho! The Lure of Yarn

The best part of crocheting is the yarn. Crocheting and knitting have recently encountered a renaissance, thanks in part to technological advances in the yarn world. New machinery produces exciting yarns mixed with bobbles, fringes, and a seemingly endless combination of fibers. Innovative chemicals and creative spinning processes produce techno yarns, microfiber, Tencel, viscose, and softer wools, alpacas, and mohair. Agricultural advancements have generated yarn made from bamboo, soy, and corn, and resulted in more refined cottons and linens. This lesson is an overview of all things yarn: how yarn is wound (a.k.a. "put up"), how to read a yarn label, yarn weight, colors, and fibers.

Hank, Skein, Ball? Unraveling Yarn Lingo

If you've been "hankering" to learn the language of yarn, here's the lowdown. Yarn is packaged in three ways: hanks, skeins, or balls.

A *ball* is just what it sounds like, a ball shape.

A *skein* (pronounced **skeyn**) is a longer, machine-wound bundle.

A *hank* is wound in a long loop. Many hand-dyed and luxury yarns are packaged this way.

The Skein Game

Which end of the yarn do I pull? Years ago, it used to be that most skeins of yarn were wound on standard machinery and you could pull from the center. Today, as the yarns available to us have vastly improved, so has the machinery. Most balls and skeins now pull from the outside. Keep your yarn in a tote or basket to keep it from rolling around on the floor.

hank

ball

skein

FIBER CONTENT Knowing what the yarn is spun from will help you predict the drape of the finished garment and how to care for it. Check to make sure it is not an allergenic fiber for the wearer (some people have wool or silk allergies, for example) and to see if it's appropriate for the project you have in mind.

WEIGHT The weight is usually given in grams or ounces (and sometimes both), and this helps determine how much yarn is needed for a project. Most yarns come in 50- to 100-gram balls or skeins. Years ago, before there was such a large variety of yarn available, patterns were written noting how many grams or ounces of yarn were needed to complete a project. Since there are so many different thicknesses of yarn available today, one 50-gram ball of yarn may have only 58 yards to a ball while another ball of the same weight may have more than 200 yards to a ball. Today most patterns will use yardage and yarn thickness, rather than weight, to determine how much yarn is needed for a project.

Get the 411 on Yarn Labels

There is a lot of valuable information on the yarn label. It's a good idea to keep a journal or notebook of your projects and include the yarn label for reference.

THE NAME OF THE YARN Helpful to know if you ever want to crochet with the yarn again or need to purchase more to finish your project.

NAME OF THE YARN MANUFACTURER Believe it or not, there are hundreds of yarn manufacturers and distributors. Often they choose the same names for their yarns, so it is a good idea to know the name of the company as well as the name of the yarn.

YARDAGE This is some of the most important information on the label. It helps you determine how much yarn you need to complete a project. Some labels note the yardage in yards while others give the information in meters. Most patterns will tell you how much yarn you need for your project in yards. Here is a quick way to figure out the conversion in your head. These measurements aren't exact, but they do the trick!

• To convert yards to meters, subtract 10%. For example, if the ball is 100 yards, 10% would be 10 yards, so your total is roughly 90 meters.

• To covert meters to yards, add 10%. For example, if the ball is 100 meters, 10% would be 10 meters, so your total is roughly 110 yards.

COLOR CODE AND DYE LOT Yarn shades are usually assigned a color number and a dye lot number. A batch of yarn dyed at the same time will have the same dye lot number. When yarn is dyed by the manufacturer, especially with hand dyes, they can vary quite a bit from batch to batch. When you purchase the yarn for a project, it is important to check the dye lot on all the balls of yarn to make sure they are all the same. If not, you could end up with a varied colored patch in the middle of your garment where the odd ball was used.

TENSION (GAUGE) AND HOOK SIZE This is the suggested tension the manufacturer suggests using for the yarn and will usually note how many stitches are worked over 1" or over 4". It also

CHEEP TRICKS

Here's a helpful solution to a common problem! What happens if you forget to check the dye lots of the yarn and you accidentally purchase two different dye lots? The Chicks say, "Think zebra stripes!" Work two or four rows, then work a second ball for two or four rows. Just keep alternating the two dye lots evenly throughout the project and they will blend beautifully!

notes the hook size used to get that gauge. This information is just a reference point for determining if the yarn will work with the project you want to make.

Get the Skinny on Yarn Weight

Yarns come in a variety of weights, which simply means the thickness of the yarn. The weights are determined by how many stitches it takes to crochet over 4". Generally speaking, the thinner the yarn, the more stitches per inch. The thicker the yarn, the fewer stitches per inch.

LACE weight yarns are the thinnest of the bunch and usually crocheted on larger hooks for lacy, openwork patterns.

SUPER FINE and **FINE** yarns are most often used for intricate projects such as socks, baby garments, and lace, to name a few.

LIGHT WORSTED, or **DK**, weight yarns are thicker than fingering weight yarn but not as thick as worsted. They are usually used for summer-weight garments, shawls, and baby items.

MEDIUM WEIGHT yarns, e.g., **WORSTED** and **ARAN** weight yarns, are the most popular thickness and are popular for sweaters, blankets, hats, mittens, and many felting projects.

BULKY and **SUPER BULKY** yarns are the thickest of the group. Some, at one stitch per inch, are often suggested for sweaters, scarves, afghans, and more. If you want a really fast project, then patterns requiring these yarns will most likely be the ones you want to head for.

This information is not ironclad, but it is helpful to give a range so you can head toward the right weight when choosing a yarn to go with a specific pattern you want to crochet.

 0 LACE: Fingering 10-count crochet thread (33-40 sts to 4")

 1 SUPER FINE: Sock, fingering, and baby weight yarns (27-32 sts to 4")

 2 FINE: Sport, baby weight yarns (23-26 sts to 4")

 3 LIGHT: DK, light worsted weight yarns (21-24 sts to 4")

 4 MEDIUM: Worsted, afghan, aran weight yarns (16-20 sts to 4")

 5 BULKY: Chunky, craft weight yarns (12-15 sts to 4")

 6 SUPER BULKY: Bulky, roving weight yarns (4-11 sts to 4")

Feel the Love: The Chicks Love Fibers

The art of crochet is all about the fiber. As you will soon find out, nothing feels better than yarn. Choosing just the right material for your project can make all the difference in its final look. A sweater crocheted in cashmere, for example, is going to have a completely different drape than one made out of mohair, silk, or even acrylic. Getting familiar with the outcome of the particular fibers will help you choose just the right one for your project.

NATURAL ANIMAL FIBERS

WOOL Spun into a wide variety of thicknesses and textures, wool, which is provided by several different breeds of sheep, has long been a popular fiber for crocheters because it is warm and breathable, accepts dye well, and is very resilient.

CASHMERE This fiber comes from the soft undercoat of cashmere goats. It's an ultra-luxurious yarn that is very soft, light, and warm.

ALPACA The coats of these South American animals produce very soft, silky, and luxurious yarn.

The softest comes from baby alpacas. The allergens found in the lanolin in lamb's wool are nonexistent in the alpaca, making it a great choice for those with wool allergies. The Chicks' best-kept secret: Since alpaca doesn't have the "street credibility" of cashmere, it is usually about one third the price.

LLAMA tends to be a bit courser than alpaca and is often used for bulkier (and warmer) garments. Like alpaca it is nonallergenic and lanolin-free. It is available in twenty-two natural shades but doesn't accept dye as easily as wool.

MOHAIR Provided by the Angora goat, mohair is a very lofty and fuzzy yarn that is usually crocheted very loosely and provides a lot of warmth. The finest mohair is kid mohair.

SILK Produced by silkworm larvae, it is light, smooth, and comfortable. There are many types of silkworms that produce different types of silk. Since silk does not have much stretch, it is hard to crochet with it alone; it is usually combined with other fibers such as wool or cashmere.

Other interesting animal fibers that are available in yarn include **ANGORA**, **CAMEL**, and **BUFFALO**.

NATURAL PLANT FIBERS

COTTON The use of this in garments dates back to ancient times. Breathable and absorbent yarn, it is ideal for hot weather. Mercerized cotton is treated with chemicals to make it shinier, silkier, and more durable. It also allows the cotton to accept dyes better and makes it mildew resistant.

BAMBOO is the new kid on the block, made from the pulp of the bamboo grass. It has a drape similar to silk—light and strong—and is nonallergenic.

LINEN comes from the flax plant. Cool and moisture resistant, it is great for summer clothing.

MAN-MADE FIBERS

Man-made fibers and those created by way of chemical processes include nylon, viscose, rayon, acrylic, and polyester. Man-made fibers, also known as synthetics, aren't as undesirable as they once were; but technological improvements have paved the way for synthetics to be softer, accept dye better, and pill less. Some yarns are composed of natural fibers—the cellulose from plants—and then turned into yarn using man-made processes. Some of these "techno fibers" include rayon, viscose, and even corn fiber.

BLENDS

Blends are a combination of different types of natural and/or manmade yarns. These yarns take the best properties from both yarns and combine them to make something completely fabulous. You may find a silk/wool blend or a cotton/acrylic blend. Try working with a few different types of blends—you may end up liking them more than pure yarns.

Choosing Yarn Color

The range of colors available today has never been greater. This feast for the eyes is usually what draws a person to a particular yarn. Everyone perceives color a bit differently. And just as some favor chocolate over vanilla ice cream, there are many "flavors" of yarn to suit your taste.

Which Comes First, the Pattern or the Yarn?

Like the age-old chicken-and-egg dilemma, where do you start when looking for a project? Go into a yarn shop and browse. Anything can spark your imagination—a beautiful color, the drape of a wrap, an interesting stitch, or the styling of a sweater. No one way to shop for a project is right or wrong; you will develop the best way that works for you. Sometimes you find a yarn you just have to work with, so you search for a pattern to do it justice. Other times you find a pattern you adore and seek out the right yarn to coordinate with it.

The options! The possibilities! This artistic process is an exciting step in crocheting. Learn to let your creative juices flow!

A Note on Yarns Used in This Book

Yarn is a lot like fashion. Some yarns are traditional and some are trendy. Some yarns have been around for fifty years (from back when Grandma crocheted) while others hang around for only a few seasons. While writing this book, we tried to stick with some of the more traditional yarns in hopes that they will be available for quite a while. However, trends change and some yarns are eventually discontinued and replaced by newer yarns. In all of the designs, we noted not only the name of the yarn and the manufacturer, but also the yarn content and the gauge. This will allow you to substitute yarns, if necessary.

Size Does Matter: Crochet Hooks

Crochet hooks come in a variety of widths, from skinny as a toothpick to thick as a broomstick. These varying widths will determine how large the stitches are. Simply put, the smaller the hook, the smaller the stitches; the larger the hook, the larger the stitches. Most hooks today are measured in U.S. standard sizes (using letters) and millimeters. However, over the years different countries have adopted their own crochet hook-sizing standards. Some use a letter, some use a number, and still others use millimeters. The chart opposite will help make sense of the hook size standards.

THE ANATOMY OF A CROCHET HOOK

A crochet hook is made up of five main parts:
POINT: The end used to insert the hook into the next chain or stitch.

CROCHET HOOK SIZES

METRIC	UNITED STATES
2.25 mm	B/1
2.75 mm	C/2
3.25 mm	D/3
3.5 mm	E/4
3.75 mm	F/5
4.0 mm	G/6
4.5 mm	7
5.0 mm	H/8
5.5 mm	I/9
6.0 mm	J/10
6.5 mm	K/10.5
8.0 mm	L/11
9.0 mm	M/N/13
10.0 mm	N/P/15
11.5 mm	P/16
15.0 mm	P/Q
16.0 mm	Q
19.0 mm	S

THROAT: The notch in the hook that catches the yarn.

SHANK: The area that holds the loops you're working with and determines the size of the stitches.

THUMB REST: The area where the thumb and finger grip the hook so you can rotate the hook and maintain balance.

HANDLE: The end of the hook that usually rests in the palm of the hand.

It's in the Bag: The Chicks' Tools Checklist

As you begin your first project you'll only need a crochet hook, yarn, scissors, and a finishing needle to weave in the yarn ends. Eventually you will need to fill your yarn bag with a few other necessities. Here are some of the tools you may want to stock up on and a brief explanation of why you'll need them.

FINISHING NEEDLES: For seaming, finishing, and weaving in yarn ends.

SCISSORS: Keep a sharp pair on hand for trimming yarn ends.

SPLIT RING MARKERS: Slip these markers right onto a stitch to help keep track of the beginning of rounds or to mark a stitch.

TAPE MEASURE: Essential for measuring a gauge swatch and the progress of your project.

COUNTER: Handy for keeping track of rows while crocheting.

SEAMING PINS: Help hold your project in place while sewing seams.

PAPER AND PENCIL: Necessary for keeping project notes.

TOTE BAG: To keep all your tools in one handy spot.

Crochet Patterns: Recipes for Success

Imagine you are about to bake a cake. You need to follow a recipe, use the right ingredients, set the proper oven temperature, and measure for the right serving size in order for the cake to come out properly. Now consider your crochet pattern the same way. To make it work, you'll need the right materials, the correct gauge, accurate measurements, and an understanding of the instructions for a successful outcome.

- The "recipe" (skill level). Is the pattern designed for an apprentice or a master chef?
- What "ingredients" (materials) will you need to whip up this tasty morsel?
- "Serving size" (completed measurements). Make the right amount for the number of guests, or, in the case of a crochet pattern, the right size garment for the wearer.
- What "temperature" (gauge) will the chef use to bake the cake? Remember, just as temperature varies from oven to oven, gauge varies from crocheter to crocheter!
- Finally, follow the instructions for putting it all together. Just as baking may have some interesting terms and abbreviations, so does crocheting. Once you become accustomed to reading them, the better "chef" crocheter you'll be!

SKILL LEVEL

Projects are usually delegated a skill level. Oftentimes we see crocheters dive (or get pushed) into projects that are too difficult. They get overwhelmed and frustrated, and give up a great hobby before they've had a chance to enjoy it. All of the designs in this book are Beginner or Advanced Beginner. They are easy not because we want to insult your intelligence (after all, you were smart enough to buy this book!). They are easy because we want you to be able to master each technique before moving on to the next.

You'll find you'll make fewer mistakes, work faster, and become more confident in your work if you take it step by step.

HOW DO I KNOW MY SKILL LEVEL?

While we stick to beginner patterns in this book, here are some of the skill ratings you may come across in other patterns:

BEGINNER: Projects for first-time crocheters. These projects use single crochet (the most basic stitch) and require minimal finishing skills.

ADVANCED BEGINNER: Projects use basic stitches and may include repetitive stitch patterns, simple color changes, and simple shaping and finishing techniques.

INTERMEDIATE: Projects using a variety of techniques, such as basic lace patterns or color patterns, mid-level shaping, and finishing techniques.

EXPERIENCED: Projects with intricate stitch patterns, techniques, and dimension, such as non-repeating patterns, multicolor techniques, fine threads, small hooks, detailed shaping, and refined finishing techniques.

MATERIALS

Patterns always indicate what type of yarn should be used and how much you will need for your project as well as the recommended hook size. See The Chicks' Tools Checklist (page 21) for other materials you will need.

COMPLETED MEASUREMENTS

Patterns usually include completed measurements for the project. For a bag or scarf this will

be the finished length, width, and depth (for bags); for a garment, the finished bust or chest size is usually given. A simple trick is to measure a great-fitting sweater that you already have in your closet and use those measurements as a guide to choosing your size.

FIND YOUR SIZE!

The first few projects in this book do not require sizing. But soon enough you will be crocheting garments, and you will find that designers don't always make "one size fits all" patterns; they include several sizes to allow the proper fit. For convenience and to save space, one pattern is written for all sizes. Size changes will be noted in corresponding order throughout the pattern. For example, let's say you want to make a sweater for yourself and you wear a size medium. The pattern will print size information like this: "Sizes: Small (**Medium**, Large, X-Large)". To match the garment to your size—Medium—you will follow the corresponding first number in parentheses throughout the pattern, like so: "ch 23 (**25**, 27, 29)". So instead of working 23 stitches (size Small), you work 25 for size Medium, 27 for a Large, and so on. It helps to go through the pattern before you begin your project and circle all your size numbers with a pencil. If no varying sizes are noted, the information is the same for all sizes.

Crochet Lingo

Crochet patterns are written using many different abbreviations and terms, which save space and create a shorthand that is easier to read. It's a good idea to become familiar with some of the basic terms before you begin any pattern.

PARENTHESIS ( ): Usually determines stitches worked in a cluster. These stitches are worked in the same stitch.

INSERT HOOK INTO NEXT STITCH: This means insert the hook into the top of the next stitch from the PREVIOUS row.

DRAW UP A LOOP: After you yarn over the hook (see page 28), you will then pull the hook through the stitch.

SC IN EACH SC: Make a single crochet into the next single crochet stitch from the PREVIOUS row.

REPEAT FROM * TO * ACROSS: A pattern may state: "*Work 2 dc in next sc*. Repeat from * to * across." This means you go back to the first asterisk and repeat the pattern between the asterisks until you reach the end of the row.

INCREASE EVERY 4TH ROW: Work Rows 1, 2, and 3 in the established pattern and then increase on the 4th row.

GAUGE

The gauge indicates how many stitches and rows were crocheted by the pattern designer over 4". It is essential to match the gauge noted so that your project will have the expected outcome, especially when crocheting a garment. Read

Lesson 7, "Take a Test Drive," (page 58) to learn how to make a test swatch and measure your gauge.

ABBREVIATIONS

Why can't they write the pattern in plain English? Crochet does use a lot of abbreviations and strange punctuation. This has been done to simplify patterns for both the publisher and the crocheter. Most of the symbols are used universally, and once you start to familiarize yourself with them you'll be able to read patterns at a glance. Abbreviations are a standardized "language" of crochet to make it easier to write and to read.

Take, for example, this instruction:

ROW 1 Beginning in the second chain from the hook, work one single crochet in each single crochet across the row.

Now look at the abbreviated version:

ROW 1 Beg in second ch from hook, work 1 sc in each sc across.

This standardized method allows designers to include many sizes and lots of additional information all in one pattern. Once you get used to reading the abbreviations you'll be soaring right along. We've placed a handy Abbreviation Key next to each pattern to help familiarize you with these terms, in addition to this complete abbreviations list.

approx.	approximately
beg	begin(ing)
ch(s)	chain(s)
ch-sp	chain-space
dec	decrease
dc	double crochet
dc2tog	double crochet two stitches together
g	grams
hdc	half double crochet
inc	increase
lp(s)	loop(s)
m	meter(s)
mm	millimeter(s)
oz	ounces
rem	remaining
rep	repeat
RS	right side of your work
sc	single crochet
sc2tog	single crochet two stitches together
sk	skip
sl st	slip stitch
sp(s)	space(s)
st(s)	stitch(es)
yd	yard(s)

What Is Crochet?

Crochet is simply using yarn and a crochet hook to create a series of loops, then joining the loops together to create fabric. Crochet may be formed by working back and forth across a row or around and around.

Rule #1: Don't curb your enthusiasm!

If you are anything like us, once you've decided you want to start something, you want the "down and dirty" basics to get on your way! The other details will come later. This "crash course" chapter will teach you some of the basics, such as how to make a slip knot, a yarn over, a chain and a foundation chain, and a single crochet, and how to fasten off, to name a few. Just by learning these simple steps, you will know how to make a variety of fun and easy projects that will help you master the art of crochet.

Get a Grip: Holding the Hook

There are two popular ways to hold a crochet hook. Practice using both methods and use whichever one feels more comfortable. After a while, the hook will feel like an extension of your finger.

KNIFE HOLD

Pretend you are holding a knife, with your hand over the hook.

Nancy says: **"This one is my personal favorite. I feel like I have a lot of control with this method and can really 'dig in' and work the stitches. The best part: It allows me to crochet faster than using the pencil hold."**

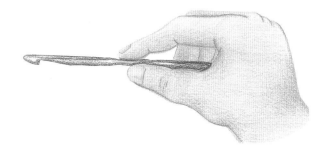

26

PENCIL HOLD

Pretend you are holding a pencil, with your hand under the hook.

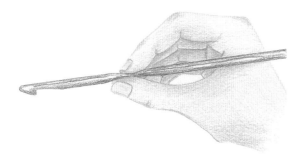

Southpaws, Don't Feel Left Out

Often we hear people complain that they can't learn to crochet because they are left-handed. Though we could only show illustrations using the right hand due to space constraints, this book is written the same for both left-handed and right-handed crocheters. Lefties, just try this easy trick: Work next to a mirror and look at any illustrations or photographs through the mirror. They will be reversed and will allow you to see exactly how stitches should be worked.

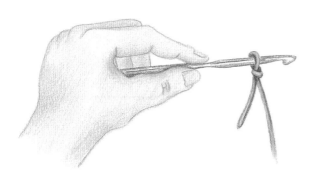

Control Yourself: Yarn Tension

One hand controls the crochet hook. If you are right-handed, the hook goes in your right hand. If you are left-handed, the hook goes in your left hand. Your other hand controls the working yarn. It is important to control the flow of the working yarn with your fingers.

Weave the yarn through your fingers and maintain a comfortable tension. The most important thing is that the yarn flows freely through your fingers and that your stitches are even. This is a technique that improves with practice. Everyone has a different method of holding the yarn that works for him or her. Some people weave the yarn in and out of their fingers; others wrap it around their pinky fingers. Try a few different ways until you find a tension that feels comfortable for you. Remember, you are learning something new; don't get frustrated if it doesn't feel comfortable right away.

Be a Little Knotty: The Slip Knot

You need to make a slip knot to begin EVERY crochet project. Leaving a 4" tail, make a loop (1). Insert the hook into the loop and catch the tail with the hook. Draw the yarn through the loop (2). Tighten the loop slightly on the hook (3). You now have the yarn attached to the hook and are ready to begin making chains.

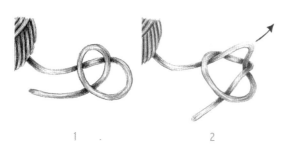

1   2

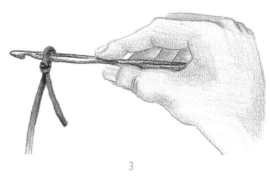

3

28

CHEEP TRICKS

All projects begin with a slip knot, but you won't find this information stated in a pattern. It is always assumed you know to make a slip knot before starting a project.

Yarn Over (yo)

The movement of yarn over is fundamental to crochet and refers to passing the hook under the yarn and catching it with the hook. Simply put, from the back, bring the yarn up and over the front of the hook, catching the yarn in the hook's throat. See accompanying illustration for making a chain.

Chain and Foundation Chain

We mentioned a bit earlier that crochet is simply the process of creating and joining loops to make fabric. Just as a house needs a foundation on which to build, so do crochet stitches. We call it the foundation chain—the row of chains upon which the next and all other rows are built.

Make a Chain (ch)

To begin a chain, grasp the base of the slip knot, yarn over, and draw the yarn through the loop on the hook. You've just made your first chain!

Repeat this technique to make a row of chains. Move your thumb and finger up the chain, keeping it close to the hook. This will be the foundation for your first row of crochet. When beginning a project, the pattern will usually state how many chains you should make. The pattern will state, for example, "Chain 10." This means to make a slip knot and place it on the hook. Then do a series of 10 chains to make your Chain 10.

Counting Chains

Notice that there are two sides to your foundation chain. The front looks like a series of hearts or a braid (1). The back looks like a series of little ridges (2). To count the chains, always count the chains from the front. Never count the slip knot or the chain that is on the hook, which is known as the working chain. When counting chains always begin counting at the chain closest to the hook. A pattern will state how many chains to make.

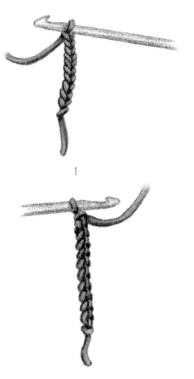

1

2

Single Crochet (sc)

This is the most basic of the crochet stitches and the one you will see most often when starting a project. Begin by making a slip knot and a foundation chain. For practice, make a slip knot and try a foundation chain of 10 chains. Insert the hook into the second chain from the hook, yarn over, pull up a loop (2 loops on hook), yarn over and draw through both loops on the hook (1). You have just made 1 single crochet (2). Continue working 1 single crochet in each chain across the row. Remember: Don't crochet in the slip knot. You should have 9 single crochet stitches. Congratulations! You have just completed your first row of single crochet.

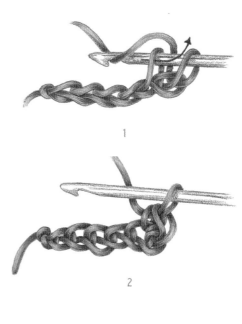

1

2

Slip Stitch (sl st)

The slip stitch is primarily used to join ends of rows or rounds or to move across the row without adding height. Begin by making a slip knot and a foundation chain. Insert hook into the second chain from the hook, yarn over and draw through both the chain and the loop on the hook. You have just made your first slip stitch.

Turning Chains (t-ch)

In order to work your next row and have the edges be the appropriate height to match your stitches, you need to make turning chains at the beginning of a row. Think of them as the little ladders of the crochet world. When you are ready to begin a new row you will need to make a turning chain as tall as the stitches in that row. A pattern will usually state how many chains you should make at the end (or beginning) of a row. This is handy information if you want to make a project on your own. For example, if you want to crochet a scarf in double crochet, you will need to chain 3 at the end of each row.

To begin the next row you will need to make a turning chain to add height. Chain 1 (just as you would make a chain for a foundation chain) and turn your work. You will now work back across

the row you just crocheted. Notice the row of braids or hearts in the row you just completed. This is where you will work your next row. Skip the turning chain and make 1 single crochet in the first single crochet. You will work all stitches in this row and hereafter going under the heart instead of through it. Continue working 1 single crochet in each single crochet across the row.

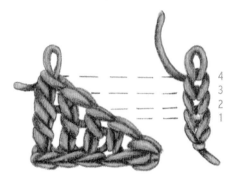

As a general rule, the following chart shows the corresponding number of turning chains to coordinate with the basic crochet stitches.

Slip Stitch	0
Single Crochet	1
Half Double Crochet	2
Double Crochet	3
Treble Crochet	4

CHEEP TRICKS

All of the patterns in this book (and most other patterns) will state how many turning chains to make at the end (or beginning) of a row.

Horse of a Different Color

The technique for changing yarn colors or adding a new ball of yarn is the same. We'll walk you through it.

CHANGING COLORS OR ADDING A NEW BALL OF YARN

Working in double crochet, with the original color, yarn over and insert the hook into the next stitch, yarn over and draw up a loop (3 loops on hook), yarn over and draw through next 2 loops on the hook. Drop the first color. Now using the new color, loop the yarn over the hook and draw it through both loops on the hook. Continue working using new yarn. Do not knot the ends of the yarn together. This is not necessary in crochet. Instead, weave in the yarn ends for a clean, tidy finish (see "Weaving in Yarn Ends" below).

This technique is also used when joining another skein of the same color. It is similar for working in single, half double, and triple crochet stitches. Start the stitch with the old color or skein and finish the stitch with the new color.

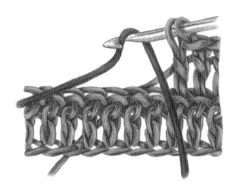

At the End of Your Rope? How to End a Project

FASTEN OFF

To end your pieces, cut the yarn from the ball, leaving approximately a 4" tail. Yarn over and draw the tail through the loop on the hook and tighten. This is the best method to fasten off each project.

WEAVING IN YARN ENDS

The easiest way to hide those dangling yarn tails once you've completed a project is to weave them into the piece. To begin, thread a yarn needle with the yarn end. With the wrong side (the side of your project that won't show) facing, weave the needle through several stitches, hiding the yarn end inside the loops of the stitches. Clip the remaining yarn end closely and check your work from the front side to be sure yarn ends are not showing through.

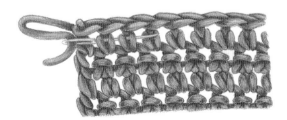

She's Come Undone: Fixing Mistakes

Slipups are common in crochet, but it's very easy to correct them. Pull out the yarn back to where you made the mistake. Then simply insert your hook back into the working loop and continue crocheting.

CHEEP TRICKS

....

Sometimes you may lose or add stitches without realizing it. To avoid getting too far into the project before finding that you don't have the right amount of stitches, it is wise to get into the habit of counting your stitches every couple of rows. This will allow you to correct your errors much more easily and cause a little less frustration.

EXTRA STITCHES

As we mentioned before, it's good to keep counting your stitches to make sure you are on track. Occasionally you will find you've added or skipped a stitch or two. There are several reasons why this happens. Often it's a result of not being able to identify stitches. You may have worked back into the same stitch or worked a stitch in the turning chain. Whatever the case may be, the more comfortable you become with crocheting, the fewer mistakes you'll make; and if you do make a mistake, you'll have that much more confidence to fix it.

WHEN YOU REACH A KNOT IN THE YARN

Nobody loves finding a knot in the middle of a ball of yarn, but occasionally you will find one or two. Do not continue crocheting with this yarn; it could unravel, and you'll end up with holes in the middle of your project.

When you find a knot, back out a couple of stitches so you have approximately 6-8" of yarn before the knot. Cut the knot out of the ball and pick up the new end and join it as if you are joining a new ball of yarn (see page 31). Weave in the yarn ends later for a secure finish.

| chicks' slit-top felted bag |

completed measurements

14" x 19" before felting

Approximately 10" x 14" after felting (expect your bag to shrink by about one third its original size)

materials

240 yd/219 m medium weight wool for felting in black

Size L/11 (8.0 mm) crochet hook

Finishing needle

SAMPLE SHOWN WAS CROCHETED USING MANOS DEL URUGUAY "WOOL" (3.5 OZ/100 G, 138 YD/ 126 M PER BALL; 100% PURE WOOL) IN BLACK.

abbreviation key

ch	chain
sc	single crochet
st(s)	stitch(es)

gauge

10 sts to 4" on size L (8.0 mm) hook or size needed to obtain gauge

Bag Panels (make 2)

Ch 45

ROW 1 Work 1 sc in second ch from hook and in each ch across—44 sc.

ROW 2 Ch 1 and turn. Work 1 sc in each sc across.

Repeat Row 2 for another 54 rows. You should have 56 rows total.

Begin handle shaping as follows:

ROW 1 Ch 1 and turn. Work 1 sc in each of next 16 sc. Set down ball of yarn. Skip next 12 sts. Attach a new ball of yarn and work 1 sc in each of next 16 sc.

ROW 2 Ch 1 and turn. Work 1 sc in each of next 16 sc. Set down ball of yarn. Pick up other ball, ch 1 and work 1 sc in each of next 16 sc on other side.

ROW 3 Ch 1 and turn. Work 1 sc in each of next 16 sc. Set down ball of yarn. Pick up other ball, ch 1 and work 1 sc in each of next 16 sc on other side.

CHICK FEED

In this project you will practice the techniques you just learned: making a slip knot, chains and foundation chains, and single crochet. You will also try counting stitches and rows. We also incorporated a really fun technique called "felting," which is covered step-by-step in Lesson 10 (page 75). You will actually be shrinking your completed bag after you crochet it! The best part—felting "melts" away any imperfections!

BEGINNER

ROW 4 Ch 1 and turn. Work 1 sc in each of next 16 sc. Ch 12. Work 1 sc in each of next 16 sc.

ROW 5 Ch 1 and turn. Work 1 sc in each sc and ch across—44 sc.

ROW 6 Ch 1 and turn. Work 1 sc in each sc across—44 sc.

Repeat Row 6 another 6 times.

Fasten off and weave in all yarn ends.

FINISHING

Now it's time to join the sides together to make the bag. You will simply hold both handbag panels together, attach yarn at a top corner, and join sides with a slip stitch. Next work a row of single crochet around the edges of the panels, down one side, across the bottom, and up the other side. Be sure you insert your hook through the thickness of both panels. Fasten off and weave in all yarn ends.

Felting the bag is your last step; see Lesson 10 on page 75 for detailed instructions.

FLY THE COOP!
For embellishment we added a bow crafted from wire-edged ribbon. Try leaving the bag plain and decorating with a few pins or a large button or even the crocheted flower shown in Lesson 17 (page 118).

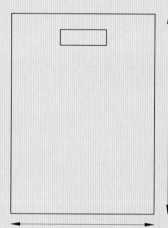

19" before felting
14" after felting

14" before felting
10" after felting

| laguna felted crochet hook case |

completed measurements

Approximately 17" x 9" before felting

Approximately 13" x 6.5" after felting

materials

120 yd/110 m medium weight wool for felting in turquoise (A)

120 yd/110 m medium weight wool for felting in purple (B)

120 yd/110 m medium weight wool for felting in green (C)

Size L/11 (8.0 mm) crochet hook

Finishing needle

SAMPLE WAS CROCHETED USING MANOS DEL URUGUAY "WOOL" (3.5 OZ/100 G, 138 YD/126 M PER BALL; 100% PURE WOOL) IN AQUA, RASPBERRY, AND CITRIC.

abbreviation key

ch   chain

sc   single crochet

st(s)   stitch(es)

gauge

11 sts and 14 rows to 4" over single crochet on size L/11 (8.0 mm) hook or size needed to obtain gauge

Case

Ch 48

ROW 1   Work 1 sc in second ch from hook and in each ch across.

ROW 2   Ch 1 and turn. Work 1 sc in each sc across.

Repeat Row 2 another 8 times. You should have 10 rows total.

Change to yarn B and repeat Row 2 3 times.

Change to yarn C and repeat Row 2 6 times.

Change to yarn B and repeat Row 2 3 times.

Change to yarn A and repeat Row 2 10 times.

Fasten off and weave in all yarn ends.

CHICK FEED
Now that you are a crocheter, you need a place to store your tools. This compact little case will keep your notions and hooks right at your fingertips. This bag is so simple to make—it's all single crochet. You'll get to practice changing colors, and any imperfections melt away when it's felted.

BEGINNER

MAKE TIES

Attach yarn at middle of side. Ch 30, turn and work 1 sc in each ch across. Fasten off and weave in all yarn ends. Repeat for opposite side.

Finishing

Follow the felting instructions given in Lesson 10 (page 75).

Once piece is dry, measure length and width.

Cut fabric to match. With right side facing up, fold all sides under ³⁄₈″ and press with an iron. Cut another piece of fabric the same width but half the length. Again fold all sides under ³⁄₈″ and press. Place shorter segment over bottom half of larger panel. Sew into place around sides and bottom. You will now have one large pocket. To create smaller pockets, beginning at the bottom edge of larger pocket, sew separate vertical seams to top edge of pocket. We spaced our pockets at varying widths to accommodate different hook sizes. Sew fabric onto felted case. We used a sewing machine to sew all the fabric onto the case, but you can just as easily use handstitching.

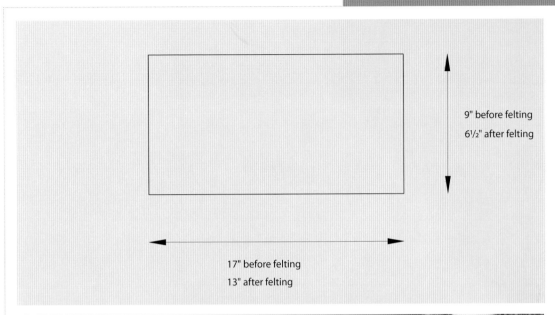

9" before felting
6½" after felting

17" before felting
13" after felting

OH MY, HOW YOU'VE GROWN!

Crochet Stitches

Now that you've mastered single crochet, you'll find that even though it's a very nice stitch, it's somewhat utilitarian and stiff. So let's move on. The following stitches are simply a variation of single crochet; you will add an extra yarn over or two and draw through loops. These extra steps result in stitches that are taller than single crochet. A half double crochet is a little taller than a single crochet; and a double crochet is just as it sounds, twice the height of a single crochet. These additional stitches become softer and more relaxed and result in an elegantly draped garment overall.

Half Double Crochet (hdc)

Begin by making a slip knot and a foundation chain. Yarn over, insert the hook into the third chain from the hook (1), yarn over and pull up a loop (now 3 loops on hook), yarn over and draw through all 3 loops on hook (2). You have just made 1 half double crochet. Continue working 1 half double crochet in each chain across. Remember: Don't crochet in the slip knot. At the end of the row you will need to make a turning chain to be able to work the next row. So chain 2 and turn your work. This turning chain counts as the first stitch in the next row. (Note: This rule

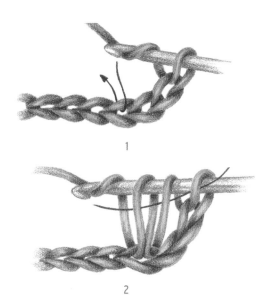

1

2

applies to all stitches except single crochet.) Skip the first half double crochet and make 1 double crochet in the next half double crochet (go under the heart to make the stitch). Continue working 1 half double crochet in each stitch across the row. At the end of the row work 1 half double crochet in the turning chain.

Double Crochet (dc)

Begin by making a slip knot and a foundation chain. Yarn over, insert the hook into the fourth chain from the hook (1), yarn over and pull up a loop (3 loops on hook). Yarn over and draw through first 2 loops on hook (2). Yarn over again and draw through last 2 loops on hook (3). You have just made 1 double crochet. Continue working 1 double crochet in each chain across. Remember: Don't crochet in the slip knot. At the end of the row you will need to make a turning chain to work your next row. Chain 3 and turn your work. This turning chain counts as the first stitch in the next row. Skip the first double crochet and make 1 double crochet in the next double crochet (go under the heart to make the stitch). Continue working 1 double crochet in each stitch across the row. At the end of the row work 1 double crochet in the turning chain.

2

3

Feeling a Little Loopy: Working in Front or Back Loops of a Stitch

Occasionally a pattern will ask you to work a stitch in the front or back of a loop. Stitches are made exactly the same way, with one exception. Instead of going UNDER the heart of the stitch from the previous row, you go THROUGH the heart of the stitch and grasp the front loop or back loop only.

A pattern is usually worded like this: "Work 1 single crochet in next single crochet in BACK LOOP only." This is how you actually work the stitch: Insert the hook into the next stitch going around the back loop only, yarn over and pull up a loop, yarn over and draw through both loops on the hook.

1

purple haze fingerless gloves

size
One size fits most

completed measurements
7" x 6"

materials
95 yd/87 m light chunky weight mohair in purple

Size H/8 (5.0 mm) crochet hook

Finishing needle

SAMPLE WAS CROCHETED USING ARTFUL YARNS "HEAVENLY" (1.75 OZ/50 G, 95 YD/87 M PER BALL; 45% MOHAIR, 35% NYLON, 15% ACRYLIC, 5% METALLIC) IN DEEP PURPLE.

abbreviation key
ch   chain

hdc   half double crochet

st(s)   stitch(es)

gauge
16 sts to 4" over hdc on size H/8 (5.0 mm) hook or size needed to obtain gauge

Gloves (make 2)

Ch 30

ROW 1   Work 1 hdc in third ch from hook and in each ch across.

ROW 2   Ch 1 and turn. Work 1 hdc in each hdc in BACK LOOPS only.

Repeat Row 2 until panel measures 6" from the beginning.

Fasten off and leave a 12" tail.

THUMB OPENING
Fold in half, joining beginning and ending edges. Using tail and horizontal mattress stitch (see page 151), sew seam 4" up from bottom and 1" down from top, leaving approximately a 2" thumb opening. Fasten off. Weave in all yarn ends.

CHICK FEED
Practice your half double crochet and working in back loops with this project. These gloves are crocheted from side to side to create a crocheted rib. They work up so quickly you'll want to make them for everyone you know!

ADVANCED BEGINNER

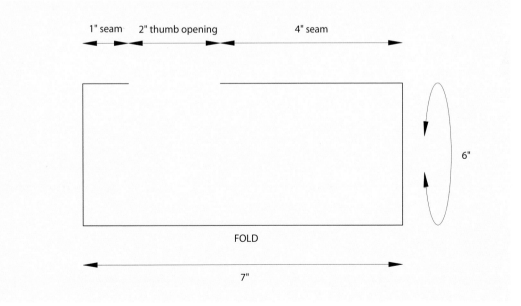

1" seam   2" thumb opening   4" seam

6"

FOLD

7"

girls' night out triangle wrap

size
One size fits most

completed measurements
Approximately 60" x 26"

materials
300 yd/274 m medium weight ribbon yarn in celadon green

Size K/10.5 (6.5 mm) crochet hook

Finishing needle

SAMPLE WAS CROCHETED USING COLINETTE "GIOTTO" RIBBON YARN (3.5 OZ/100 G, 155 YD/142 M PER HANK; 50% COTTON, 40% RAYON, 10% NYLON) IN MOSS.

abbreviation key

ch	chain
lp(s)	loop(s)
sc	single crochet
st(s)	stitch(es)

gauge
12 sc to 4" on size K/10.5 (6.5 mm) hook or size needed to obtain gauge

Shawl

Ch 8, join with sc to first st in ch to form a circle.

ROW 1   Ch 6, work 1 sc in circle, ch 4, 1 dc in circle.

ROW 2   Ch 6 and turn. Work 1 sc in first lp, ch 4, 1 sc in next lp, ch 4, and work 1 dc in same lp.

ROW 3   Ch 6 and turn. Work 1 sc in first lp, *ch 4, 1 sc in next lp*. Repeat from * to * across. Ch 4 and work 1 dc back into last lp.

Repeat Row 3 until panel shawl reaches desired size.

Fasten off and weave in all yarn ends.

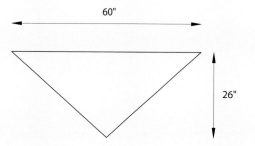

60"

26"

CHICK FEED
Make it today, wear it tonight! The shawl starts out at the bottom point and works up, allowing you to try it on as you make it and get just the right length. It's so easy it almost shapes itself! You will practice making chains and joining them with a single crochet. We crocheted this in a shiny ribbon yarn for some added nighttime sizzle.

ADVANCED BEGINNER

FLY THE COOP!
Try some of these pattern alternatives:

- Use mohair for a warmer wrap.

- Embellish with fringe along the two shorter sides. To make fringe, cut a piece of cardboard $1/2''$ longer than the desired length of your fringe. Wrap yarn around cardboard several times and cut through yarn along one edge of cardboard. Gather 2-4 strands of cut yarn; fold them in half and pull folded end through an edge stitch in the garment where you want to add your fringe. Pull the other end of the yarn through the loop and tighten.

- Make wrap a little smaller and it becomes a cute scarf. (See Lesson 6 for decreasing help, page 50.)

- Make wrap a little larger and it becomes a sexy beach sarong. (See Lesson 5 for increasing help, page 48.)

REACH FOR THE SKY

Treble Crochet (tr)

Treble crochet, also known as triple crochet, is the tallest of the five basic stitches (slip stitch, single crochet, half double crochet, double crochet, and treble crochet). It is a very long, elegant stitch, usually used in lacy, open projects.

Begin by making a slip knot and a foundation chain. Yarn over, and then yarn over again (1). Insert hook into the fifth chain from the hook, yarn over and pull up a loop (4 loops on hook), yarn over and draw through first 2 loops on hook (2), yarn over again and draw through next 2 loops on hook (3). Yarn over and draw through last 2 loops on hook (4). You have just made 1 treble crochet. Continue working 1 treble crochet in each chain across. Remember: Don't crochet in the slip knot. At the end of the row you will need to make a turning chain to work the next row. To do this, chain 4 and turn your work. You will now work back across the top of the row you just made. This turning chain counts as the first stitch in the next row. Skip the first treble crochet and make 1 treble crochet in the next treble crochet going under the heart to make the stitch. Continue working 1 treble crochet in each stitch across the row. At the end of the row work 1 treble crochet in the turning chain.

44

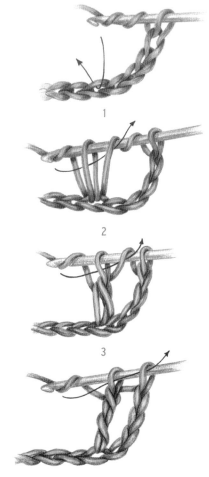

1

2

3

4

sunrise shawl

size
One size fits most

completed measurements
Approximately
9" x 50" (not including fringe)

materials

100 yd/91 m each eyelash yarn in pink and taupe (A & B)

180 yd/165 m chunky weight mohair in wheat (C)

140 yd/128 m metallic fingering weight yarn in pink (D)

140 yd/128 m ribbon yarn in soft pink (E)

Size P (11.5 mm) crochet hook

Finishing needle

SAMPLE WAS CROCHETED USING COLINETTE "GIOTTO" IN SUNRISE, COLINETTE "MOHAIR" IN BISCUIT, PLYMOUTH "COLORLASH" IN TAUPE, PLASSARD "INSOLITE" IN BLUSH, AND ROWAN "LUREX" IN PINK

abbreviation key

beg	beginning
ch	chain
lp(s)	loop(s)
sc	single crochet
st(s)	stitch(es)
t-ch	turning chain
tr	treble crochet

gauge
8 sts to 4" over sc on size P (11.5 mm) hook or size needed to obtain gauge

NOTE: THIS PATTERN CALLS FOR CHANGING YARNS AT THE END OF EVERY SECOND ROW. IT IS **NOT** NECESSARY TO CUT THE YARNS EVERY TIME COLORS CHANGE. YARN WILL BE "CARRIED" UP THE SIDE BY DROPPING THE OLD YARN AND PICKING UP NEW YARN. (BE CAREFUL NOT TO PULL TOO TIGHTLY WHEN CHANGING COLORS.)

Shawl

Using yarns A, C, and D held together at the same time, ch 19.

ROW 1 Beg in second ch from hook, work 1 sc in each ch across—18 sts.

CHICK FEED
We designed this pattern when Mary Ellen needed something to WOW a few friends. We used the long, graceful stitches of treble crochet to mimic a knitted drop-stitch design. This will test your skills working in treble crochet, making turning chains, and changing yarns.

BEGINNER

ROW 2 Ch 3 and turn (counts as first tr in row now and throughout). Sk first sc and work 1 tr in each sc across—18 sts.

ROW 3 Change to yarn E. Ch 1 and turn. Work 1 sc in each tr across and in t-ch at end of row—18 sts.

ROW 4 Ch 3 and turn. Sk first sc and work 1 tr in each sc across.

ROW 5 Change to yarns B, C, and D. Ch 1 and turn. Work 1 sc in each tr across and in t-ch at end of row.

ROW 6 Ch 3 and turn. Sk first sc and work 1 tr in each sc across.

ROW 7 Change to yarn E. Ch 1 and turn. Work 1 sc in each tr across and in t-ch at end of row.

ROW 8 Ch 3 and turn. Sk first sc and work 1 tr in each sc across.

ROW 9 Change to yarns A, C, and D. Ch 1 and turn. Work 1 sc in each tr across and in t-ch at end of row.

ROW 10 Ch 3 and turn. Sk first sc and work 1 tr in each sc across.

Repeat Rows 3 through 10 another 5 times. Panel measures approximately 50" from the beg. Fasten off and weave in all yarn ends.

Fringe

Cutting all fringe 36" long, cut 72 strands of C, 36 strands of D, and 36 strands of E.

Pick up 2 strands of C, 1 strand of D, and 1 strand of E to make 1 fringe. Fold in half to form a lp. Insert hook into first st at end of row on shawl and draw fringe lp through st. Pull tails through lp and tighten. Repeat in remaining 17 sts across and in all 18 sts at other end of shawl.

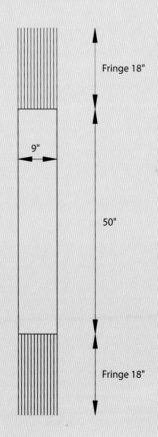

Fringe 18"

9"

50"

Fringe 18"

GIVE ME MORE

Increasing

Increasing is a method of adding stitches to do nifty things such as make a ruffle, shape sleeves on a sweater, or shape a hat, to name just a few examples. To increase, you simply work two or more stitches into one stitch in the previous row. It's as simple as that, as you'll see when you get started on this curly scarf.

How will you know when to increase? The pattern may state: "Work two single crochet in the next single crochet."

Translated into plain English, this means you'll work an increase of one single crochet. Increasing is as easy as that.

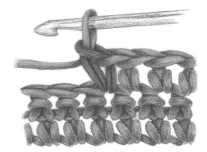

curly scarf

size
One size fits most

completed measurements
2″ x 38″

materials
110 yd/100.5 m chunky weight mohair yarn in green

Size P (11.5 mm) crochet hook

Finishing needle

SAMPLE WAS CROCHETED USING BE SWEET "BRUSHED MOHAIR" (1.75 OZ/50 G, 110 YD/100 M PER BALL; 100% BABY MOHAIR) IN ACID GREEN.

abbreviation key

beg	beginning
ch	chain
dc	double crochet
sc	single crochet
st(s)	stitch(es)

gauge
7 dc over 4″ on size P (11.5 mm) hook or size needed to obtain gauge

Scarf
Ch 66

ROW 1 Beg in second ch from hook, work 1 sc in each ch across—65 sts. Ch 1 and turn.

ROW 2 Work 2 dc in each sc across—130 sts. Ch 2 and turn.

ROW 3 Work 2 dc in each dc across—260 sts. Fasten off and weave in all yarn ends.

CHICK FEED
This is one of the easiest projects in the book. Just follow the directions and the scarf will curl by itself. Our friend Heather went to dinner at a friend's house and crocheted this scarf while there. She then presented it as a hostess gift!

BEGINNER

Decreasing

If you want your projects to take shape, you will need to learn how to decrease. This is also known as crocheting two stitches together. Decreasing is a method commonly used to shape sweaters, the toes of socks, the top of a hat, and unlimited possibilities for other items. To decrease, you work one stitch over two or three stitches in the previous row.

Decrease in Single Crochet (sc2tog)

Insert the hook into the next stitch, yarn over and pull up a loop (2 loops on hook). Now insert the hook into the next stitch, yarn over and pull up a loop (3 loops on hook), yarn over and draw through all 3 loops on the hook. You have just completed 1 single crochet decrease.

Decrease in Double Crochet (dc2tog)

Yarn over, insert the hook into the next stitch, yarn over and pull up a loop, yarn over and draw through first 2 loops on hook (2 loops remain on hook). Yarn over, now insert the hook into the next stitch, yarn over and pull up a loop, yarn over and draw through next 2 loops on hook (3 loops remain on hook), yarn over and draw through all 3 loops on hook. You have just completed 1 double crochet decrease.

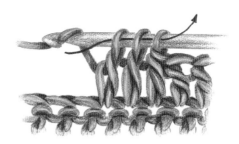

Decrease 1 Stitch (dec 1)

We just showed you the two most common ways of decreasing. When you are working some stitch patterns, a pattern may tell you to "dec 1 st." In that case, it is assumed that you will continue in the established pattern. This type of decrease is not commonly used in beginner patterns.

| leftovers diagonal scarf |

size
One size fits most

completed measurements
4 ½" x 72"

materials
300 yd/274 m worsted weight novelty yarns in various colors

Size K/10.5 (6.5 mm) crochet hook

Finishing needle

WE USED PRISM "COOL STUFF" (3.5 OZ/100 G SKEINS, 150 YD/137 M HANK; RAYON, COTTON, NYLON, POLYESTER, SILK) IN CANTINA. NOTE ON THE YARN: YOU COULD MAKE YOUR OWN LEFTOVER YARN BALL, BUT WE USED PRISM'S "COOL STUFF" YARN BECAUSE THE LEFTOVER BALL IS CREATED FOR YOU. IT'S FUN YARN TO WORK WITH BECAUSE IT IS HAND DYED AND HAND-TIED. THE YARNS CHANGE EVERY FEW YARDS, SO YOU DON'T KNOW WHAT YOU'LL BE CROCHETING WITH NEXT!

abbreviation key

ch	chain
dc	double crochet
dc2tog	double crochet two stitches together
sc	single crochet
st(s)	stitch(es)

gauge
13 sts to 4" over sc on size K/10.5 (6.5 mm) hook or size needed to obtain gauge

52

Scarf

Ch 20

ROW 1   Work 1 dc in third ch from hook and in each ch across—18 dc. (CHEEP TRICKS: Place a marker at this end of the row. That way you will always know you are at the decrease end when you are at this end.)

ROW 2   Ch 2 and turn. Dc2tog over first 2 sts, work 1 dc in each dc across to last st. Work 2 dc in last st.

ROW 3   Ch 2 and turn. Work 2 dc in first st, work 1 dc in each dc across to last 2 sts. Dc2tog over last 2 sts.

Repeat Rows 2 and 3 until panel measures desired length. Fasten off and weave in all yarn ends.

CHICK FEED
Use up all the leftover yarns from other projects. The Leftovers Scarf is worked diagonally, and it is a lot easier than it looks (we're not kidding!). You will always decrease on one side of the scarf and increase on the other.

ADVANCED BEGINNER

zigzag silk bag

CHICK FEED
We *LOVE* the construction of this bag. We crocheted a zigzag panel, folded it in half, then sewed together the side and bottom. You can crochet this using a variety of yarns, but we used a yarn made from recycled silk saris for an organic feel and rich jewel-like tones.

completed
measurements

**13" x 17"
not including strap**

materials

**320 yd/293 m light
chunky weight yarn**

**Size K/10.5 (6.5 mm)
crochet hook**

Finishing needle

WE USED HIMALAYA YARNS "TIBET"
(3.5 OZ/100 G, 80 YD/73 M PER
HANK; 100% RECYCLED SILK).

abbreviation key

beg	beginning
ch(s)	chain(s)
ch-2 sp	chain-two space
dc(s)	double crochet(s)
dc2tog	double crochet two stitches together
hdc	half double crochet
sc	single crochet
st(s)	stitch(es)

gauge
**12 sts to 4" over dc on
size K/10.5 (6.5 mm) hook
or size needed to obtain
gauge**

NOTE: SEE LESSON 11, "CHAIN GANG," (PAGE 85) FOR CHAIN-SPACE
AND CHAIN-TWO SPACE STITCH HELP.

Bag
Ch 94

ROW 1 Work 1 dc in third ch from hook and in next
20 chs, dc2tog skipping 2 chs in between dcs. Work
1 dc in each of next 20 chs, ch 2, work 1 dc in each
of next 20 chs. Dc2tog skipping 2 chs in between
dcs. Work 1 dc in each of next 20 chs and work 2 dc
in last ch.

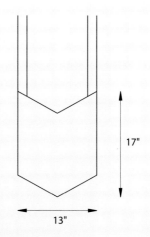

17"

13"

ADVANCED BEGINNER

ROW 2 Ch 2, turn and work 1 dc in first dc. Work 1 dc in each of next 20 dc. Dc2tog skipping 1 st between dcs. Work 1 dc in each of next 20 dcs. In next ch-2 sp work (1 dc, ch 2, 1 dc). Work 1 dc in each of next 20 dc. Dc2tog skipping 1 st between dcs. Work 1 dc in each of next 20 dcs. Work 2 dc in last st.

Repeat Row 2 until panel measures 10" from the beg.

Fasten off and weave in all yarn ends.

FINISHING

Fold panel in half lengthwise. Use horizontal mattress stitch to sew bottom seams and vertical mattress stitch to sew the sides (see Lesson 19 for finishing instructions, page 148).

Shoulder Strap

Shoulder Straps are made by attaching yarn at the high points on each side, working up to the middle of the shoulder, then sewing a seam to join the straps.

Attach yarn to top edge of bag, 5 sts BEFORE the side seam. Ch 3, work 1 dc in each of next 4 sts, in next st work (1 dc, ch 2, 1 dc), work 1 dc in each of next 5 sts.

ROW 1 Ch 2, dc2tog, 1 dc in each of next 3 sts, in ch-2 sp work (1 dc, ch 2, 1 dc), work 1 dc in each of next 3 sts, dc2tog.

Repeat Row 1 until Shoulder Strap measures 17" or to desired length. (The strap will stretch with wear, so don't overdo it!)

LAST ROW Ch 2, dc2tog, 1 hdc in each of next 3 sts, in ch-2 sp work 2 sc. Work 1 hdc in each of next 3 sts, dc2tog. Fasten off.

Attach yarn at opposite top edge, 5 sts BEFORE the ch-2 sp. Ch 3, work 1 dc in each of next 4 sts, in ch-2 sp work (1 dc, ch 2, 1 dc), work 1 dc in each of next 5 sts.

ROW 1 Ch 2, dc2tog, 1 dc in each of next 3 sts, in ch-2 sp work (1 dc, ch 2, 1 dc), work 1 dc in each of next 3 sts, dc2tog.

Repeat Row 1 until Shoulder Strap matches the other strap.

LAST ROW Ch 2, dc2tog, 1 hdc in each of next 3 sts, in ch-2 sp work 2 sc. Work 1 hdc in each of next 3 sts, dc2tog. Fasten off.

Sew strap ends together. Weave in all yarn ends.

| retro chevron stripe throw |

completed measurements
30" x 36" for baby blanket
(47" x 67" for throw)

materials
300 yd/274 m (900 yd/823 m) light chunky weight mohair in pink (A)

200 yd/183 m (600 yd/549 m) light chunky weight mohair in mocha (B)

200 yd/183 m (600 yd/549 m) light chunky weight mohair in purple (C)

Size K/10.5 (6.5 mm) crochet hook

Finishing needle

SAMPLE WAS CROCHETED USING JO SHARP "RARE COMFORT KID MOHAIR" (.88 OZ/25 G, 95 YD/87 M PER BALL; 80% KID MOHAIR, 15% POLYAMIDE) IN 604, 601, AND 603.

abbreviation key

ch	chain
ch-sp	chain-space
dc	double crochet
dc2tog	double crochet two stitches together
sk	skip
t-ch	turning chain

gauge
14 sts to 4" over dc on K/10.5 (6.5 mm) hook or size needed to obtain gauge

NOTE: SEE LESSON 11, "CHAIN GANG," (PAGE 85) FOR CHAIN-SPACE STITCH HELP.

Throw
NOTE: PATTERN IS WORKED BY ALTERNATING THE THREE COLORS EVERY 6TH ROW.

Ch 144 (224)

ROW 1 Work 1 dc in fourth ch from hook, *(ch 1, sk next ch, 1 dc in next ch) 3 times; ch 1, sk next ch, dc2tog skipping 3 chs in between dcs; (ch 1, sk next ch, 1 dc in next ch) 3 times; ch 1, sk next ch, in next ch work (1 dc, ch 3, 1 dc)*. Repeat from * to * across ending with (1 dc, ch 1, 1 dc) in last ch.

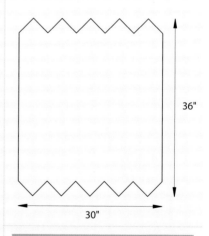

36"

30"

ADVANCED BEGINNER

ROW 2 Ch 3 and turn. (1 dc in dc, 1 dc in ch-sp) 4 times; *dc2tog skipping (ch, dc2tog, ch) between dcs; (1dc in ch-sp, 1 dc in next dc) 3 times; in ch 3-sp work (2 dc, ch 3, 2 dc); (1 dc in dc, 1 dc in ch-sp) 3 times*. Repeat from * to * across ending with (1 dc, ch 1, 1 dc) in last ch.

ROW 3 Ch 3 and turn. 1 dc in first dc, sk ch, ch 1, *(1 dc, sk 1 dc, ch 1) 3 times; dc2tog skipping (dc, dc2tog, dc) between dcs; (sk next dc, ch 1, 1 dc) 3 times, ch 1; in ch 3-sp work (1 dc, ch 3, 1 dc), ch 1*. Repeat from * to * across, ending with (1 dc, ch 1, 1 dc) in t-ch.

Repeat Rows 2 and 3 until throw measures desired length. Fasten off and weave in all yarn ends.

CHICK FEED
This isn't your grandma's afghan, but it is inspired by those groovy afghans that everyone had folded over the back of the family room couch in the 1970s. We gave it a modern feel by working an open chevron stripe out of rich kid mohair and choosing a more current colorway of soft pinks and mocha. We've also given you two size options: a quick-finishing baby blanket or a full-size throw.

Test Swatches

Though each pattern in the book offers gauge information, up to this point it wasn't really important if you made a test swatch. We wanted you to get a taste for crocheting and just relax and enjoy the process. Now we are stepping it up a notch. The projects going forward will require you to crochet a test swatch before you begin. This lesson explains why making a test swatch is so important, especially when crocheting a garment such as a sweater—it's a critical step in making sure the garment will fit!

58

What Is a Test Swatch?

When buying a car, you usually take it out for a test drive. You check that it is the right fit for you, that it's comfortable, that it serves your needs, and most of all, that it looks goooood! A test swatch is like a test drive for your crocheting. It is a sample swatch crocheted using the yarn and hook you plan to use for a project. You'll check that it's just the right fit for the pattern, that it feels good, that it serves your needs, and most of all, that it looks goooood!

How to Make a Test Swatch

1. Using your selected yarn and suggested hook size noted in the pattern, crochet a 5 x 5" test swatch.

2. To figure out how many stitches to chain, take the number of stitches noted in the pattern's gauge and add 10. For example, if the pattern states: "16 stitches and 12 rows to 4" over single crochet on size I (5.5 mm) hook," you will make a test swatch of approximately 26 stitches and in single crochet using a size I (5.5 mm) hook.

3. Lay the test swatch on a flat surface.

4. Using a ruler, count how many stitches and how many rows are in 4 inches. This will give you your gauge.

I've Made a Test Swatch, Now What?

I have the right number of stitches to match the gauge.

Go ahead and begin your project.

Help, I have too many stitches!

If you have too many stitches, your gauge is too tight; try making the swatch again using a larger hook.

Help, I don't have enough stitches!

If you have too few stitches, your gauge is too loose; try making the swatch again using a smaller hook.

Help, my stitches are uneven!

Most likely you need to work on maintaining even tension in your crocheting. Keep practicing and your tension will improve. As a new crocheter, your gauge may evolve. Often we see new crocheters begin a swatch that is extremely tight because they are a little tense. As they relax, so does their tension. As a result, the gauge swatch may be two sizes too tight at the beginning and really loose at the middle and end. You need to be consistent in your stitches for the project to work to your expectations.

Test Swatch Project Ideas

CROCHET SCRAPBOOK

Don't throw away your test swatch! Swatches can be excellent reference tools for future projects. Many hookers keep a "crochet scrapbook." It usually includes the test swatch, pattern, notes made while crocheting, and even a photo of the person wearing the completed garment.

SWATCH BLANKET

Save all your gauge swatches. When you've stashed enough of them, crochet them together into a blanket and donate it to charity!

UNDERSTANDING GARMENT CONSTRUCTION

Following a Garment Pattern

There are several ways to make a sweater, including bottom-up, top-down, and flat-panel construction. The bottom-up method begins at the lower edge of the sweater and requires working the front and back as one piece. The sleeves are worked separately, and then all the pieces are joined at the same time; the yoke is worked as one piece. This method is usually considered a more advanced type of garment construction. The biggest advantage to the bottom-up method is that it requires very little finishing, as there are few or no seams to sew. Top-down construction is appealing for the same reason but works the process in reverse. The garment begins at the neck, and the front and back are worked in one piece. Stitches are skipped for the sleeve openings, then resumed for the front and back, all done in one piece down to the waist. The most common method is known as flat-panel construction. That simply means panels are constructed individually in flat-panel pieces. The back, front, and sleeves are crocheted separately and then sewn together. Take a look at some of the store-bought sweaters in your closet, which were most likely made using this method.

In the following project we introduce crochet shorthand and will walk you step-by-step through making a simple vest. You will learn how to make a garment that fits, to map out your pattern, and to put those pieces together.

alex's t-shirt vest

find your size

It's time to pick the size of the garment you want to crochet. Pull out a great-fitting sweater from your closet (it can be store-bought). Lay it on a flat surface and measure it across directly under the arms. Double that number and that will be your size measurement. For example, if your sweater measures 18" across, 36" is the size you should go with. Some patterns will size their garments with ease measurements built in, claiming they will fit bust sizes 32, 34, 36, etc., but always look for the completed measurement. That is the true size of the garment when crocheted—assuming, of course, that your gauge is accurate!

sizes

Small (Medium, Large, X-Large)

completed chest measurements

32 (36, 38, 40)"

materials

400 (450, 500, 600) yd/ 366 (411, 457, 549) m worsted weight yarn, any fiber content in color of your choice

Size M/13 (9.0 mm) crochet hook

Finishing needle

Paper and pencil

SAMPLE WAS CROCHETED USING PRISM "WILD STUFF" (3.5 OZ/ 100 G, 150 YD/137 M PER HANK; RAYON, COTTON, NYLON, POLY- ESTER, SILK) IN TUMBLEWEED.

abbreviation key

beg	beginning
ch	chain
dc	double crochet
dc2tog	double crochet 2 stitches together
lp(s)	loop(s)
sc	single crochet
st(s)	stitch(es)
yo	yarn over

STITCH HELP FOR THIS PROJECT: DC2TOG WORKS AS FOLLOWS: YO AND INSERT HOOK INTO NEXT ST. YO AND PULL UP A LP. YO AND DRAW THROUGH 2 LPS ON HOOK. YO AND INSERT HOOK INTO NEXT ST. YO AND PULL UP A LP. YO AND DRAW THROUGH FIRST 2 LPS ON HOOK, YO AGAIN AND DRAW THROUGH ALL 3 LPS ON HOOK.

gauge

8 sts and 5 rows to 4" over dc on size M/13 (9.0 mm) hook. Working a test swatch is very important to ensure your garment will fit properly. Be sure to read Lesson 7, "Take a Test Drive" (page 58) and make a test swatch.

ADVANCED BEGINNER

CHICK FEED

Our friend Alex was looking for a little something she could just whip on over her T-shirt and jeans to feel a bit more pulled together. We came up with this easy-to-crochet vest. Worked in double crochet with very minimal shaping, it's a good "first sweater" project since you don't have to do much sewing and there are no sleeves. We worked this project in Prism "Stuff" just to prove a point: As long as you make this sweater in a worsted weight yarn and use the appropriate gauge, you will achieve the anticipated results. (The yarn is called "Stuff" because they've thrown in just about every type of worsted weight yarn you can think of, which makes for a very interesting ball of yarn). When choosing your yarn for the project, you can use just about any worsted weight yarn and be guaranteed that it will look great.

Back

NOTE: GARMENTS USUALLY START WITH THE BACK. THEY ARE USUALLY THE LARGEST PIECE AND, IN THIS CASE, THE EASIEST. AFTER YOU FINISH THE BACK OF THIS PROJECT, MORE THAN HALF OF YOUR GARMENT WILL BE COMPLETE.

Ch 37 (41, 43, 45)

ROW 1 Work 1 dc in third ch from hook and in each ch across–35 (39, 41, 43) dc.

ROW 2 Ch 2 and turn. 1 dc in each dc across.

Repeat Row 2 another 12 (14, 14, 12) rows from the beg. Panel should measure approximately 11 (12 ½, 12 ½, 11)" from the beg.

Begin armhole shaping as follows: Dc2tog over first 2 sts, work 1 dc in each st across to last 2 sts, dc2tog over last 2 sts–2 decreases made in this row.

NEXT ROW Ch 2 and turn. Work 1 dc in each dc across. Now read the Chicks' Crochet Shorthand.

THE CHICKS' CROCHET SHORTHAND
Time to learn crochet shorthand and how to organize your pattern information to work through your project.

WHY DO I HAVE TO LEARN CROCHET SHORTHAND?
As you advance as a crocheter, the difficulty of your projects may too. We are providing you with the tools to be able to work through the most complex stitches and garments without missing a stitch. Just as a child must learn numbers before being able to write math problems, crocheters have to become comfortable with reading a pattern and making a few projects before moving on to more advanced techniques. Now you will have several things to remember while working rows. Instead of making yourself crazy trying to keep your row/decrease information in your head, crochet shorthand is a note system that will allow you to continue crocheting as comfortably as before, even on more complex projects.

63

WHAT IS THE CHICKS' CROCHET SHORTHAND?

Let's head back to the instructions for the vest back, in particular, line two, below, which reads "Dc2tog over first 2 and last 2 sts at each end of every other row, 3 (3, 4, 4) times." In the case of the smallest size, it means that you will be decreasing at the beginning and end of every other row over a total of 6 rows. Do you think we remember all that information in our heads while crocheting? We don't! We simply write out the rows like this:

Row 1
Row 2 – dec 1 each end
Row 3
Row 4 – dec 1 each end
Row 5
Row 6 – dec 1 each end
After you complete a row, check it off. You can then set down the project, come back to it anytime, look at your notes, and know exactly where to pick up and work!

Continuing in dc, decrease on rows as follows: Dc2tog over first 2 and last 2 sts at each end of every other row 3 (3, 4, 4) times. You should have 27 (29, 29, 31) sts remaining.

Work in dc until armhole measures approximately 8 (8, 8, 9 ½)"–10 (10, 10, 12) rows. Fasten off and weave in all yarn ends.

Front (make 2)

Ch 20 (22, 23, 24)

ROW 1   Work 2 dc in third ch from hook and in each ch across.

ROW 2   Ch 2 and turn. Work 1 dc in each dc across.

Repeat Row 2 another 12 (14, 14, 12) rows from the beg. Panel should measure approximately 11 (12½, 12½, 11)" from the beg.

Begin crochet shorthand. We familiarized you with crochet shorthand while working on the Back of this project. Now you will have to shape the armhole and the neck at the same time. This is where knowing shorthand really pays off! Let's take a look at the upcoming rows:

Begin armhole shaping as follows: Dec 1 st at armhole edge of next row, then every other row 3 (3, 4, 4) times. AT THE SAME TIME begin neck shaping as follows: Dc2tog at neck edge of next 1 (2, 1, 2) rows, then every other row 5 (5, 5, 5) times.

We will use our shorthand and map out the smallest size.

ARMHOLE EDGE	ROW #	NECK EDGE
Dec 1	1	Dec 1
	2	
Dec 1	3	Dec 1
	4	

Dec 1	5	Dec 1
	6	
Dec 1	7	Dec 1
	8	
	9	Dec 1
	10	
	11	Dec 1

Place a marker at the armhole edge. Begin armhole shaping as follows: Dec 1 st at armhole edge of next row then every other row 3 (3, 4, 4) times. AT THE SAME TIME begin neck shaping as follows: Dc2tog at neck edge of next 1 (2, 1, 2) rows, then every other row 5 (5, 5, 5) times. You should have 8 (8, 8, 9) sts remaining. Work in dc until armhole measures approximately 8 (8, 8, 9 ½)"–10 (10, 10, 12) rows. Fasten off and weave in all yarn ends.

Finishing

Now you will sew your pieces together as follows:

Use horizontal mattress stitch to sew the front to back along shoulder seams. Use vertical mattress stitch to sew side seams. Refer to Lesson 19 (page 148) for help.

Weave in all yarn ends.

Evenly work 1 row of sc around edges.

FRONT TIES

Ch 31, beg in second ch from hook, work 1 sc in each ch across. Fasten off and using tails attach Tie to one front at neck edge. Make another Tie and attach on other front. Weave in all yarn ends.

65

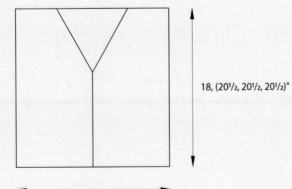

18, (20½, 20½, 20½)"

17½ (19½, 20½, 21½)"

CROCHETING IN THE ROUND

Crocheting a Tube or a Circle

Have you ever seen a weaving loom? The vertical threads on the loom (known as the "warp" threads) are held in place on the loom while the weaver moves the loose, or "weft," threads back and forth through the warp to create a panel of fabric. In our previous lessons we have worked crochet in a similar method—back and forth. What makes crochet unique is that it is more free-form than weaving or even knitting: Since you only have one stitch on the hook at a time you can go wherever you want with your next stitch—up, down, back and forth, or around and around!

In this lesson we learn how to crochet in the round. Simply put, it's like making one endless row; you keep going around and around until your project is done! What makes crocheting in the round different than crocheting back and forth is that you do not turn your work at the end of a row. Hats, mittens, skirts, one-piece sweaters, socks, and handbags are just a few of the items that you can create by this method.

66

Totally Tubular!

There are two methods of crocheting in the round: a crocheted tube and a crocheted circle. To understand a crocheted tube, let's look at the MP3 Player Sock or the Regatta Roll Brim Hat projects that follow in this lesson. We begin both of these projects with a foundation chain, but instead of working in one of the chains close to the hook, we begin in the first chain made (the one right next to the slip knot). These projects are worked around and around until you reach your desired length. In the case of the MP3 Player Sock, the bottom is then sewn shut as the final touch.

Crocheting a Circle

To understand a crocheted circle, let's look at the Smellin'-Like-a-Rose Washcloths pattern, which differs from a tube in that it is crocheted flat. In this project we begin with a small foundation chain that is joined to form a ring (1). All of the stitches in the first round are worked into this ring to form a very tight center (2). When we increase with each round, the stitches will spiral outward, creating a circle. It's helpful to mark the beginning of the rounds with a stitch marker so that you don't lose your place.

1

2

MP3 player sock

completed measurements
Approximately 4" x 2"

materials
50 yd/48 m wool or wool blend worsted weight yarn in aqua

Size H/8 (5.0 mm) crochet hook

Finishing needle

Leaving approximately a 12" tail, make a slip knot then a ch of 22.

Be careful not to twist the ch and work 1 sc in the first ch after the slip knot.

Continue working 1 sc in each ch around.

Continue working 1 sc in each sc around and around until panel measures 3 ¾" from the beg. Finish off.

Using the tail from the beg of the project, sew bottom edge using the whipstitch (see page 149). Weave in all yarn ends.

CHICK FEED

Try this quick example of crocheting a tube. You'll understand the concept as well as get a cool little player/cell phone sock. Add a few more stitches to the starting chain and it can be a small purse.

BEGINNER

| regatta rolled-brim hat |

sizes

1 year (2-3 year, 4-6 year, Adult Small, Medium, Large)

finished cap circumference

13 (15, 17, 19, 21, 23)"
Note: There will be some stretch to this hat, so these measurements are 1-2" smaller than actual head measurement.

materials

100 (100, 100, 150, 175, 200) yd/91 (91, 91, 137, 160, 183) m worsted weight yarn in moss green

Size K/10.5 (6.5 mm) crochet hook

Finishing needle

SAMPLE WAS CROCHETED USING CLASSIC ELITE "INCA ALPACA" (1.75 OZ/50 G, 109 YD/100 M PER HANK; 100% ALPACA) IN #1176.

abbreviation key

beg	beginning
ch	chain
sc	single crochet
sc2tog	single crochet two together
st(s)	stitch(es)

gauge

15 sts and 21 rows to 4" over sc on K/10.5 (6.5 mm) hook or size needed to obtain gauge

Cap

NOTE: ROUNDS ARE WORKED CONTINUOUSLY. MARK THE BEGINNING OF EACH ROUND WITH A STITCH MARKER OR SAFETY PIN. DO NOT JOIN WITH SLIP STITCH OR TURN AT THE END OF A ROUND.

Ch 49 (56, 63, 70, 77, 84)

ROUND 1   Beg in second ch from hook, work 1 sc in each ch around.

ROUND 2   Work 1 sc in each sc around.

Repeat Round 2 until panel measures 4½ (5, 5½, 6, 7, 8)" from the beg.

Shape Cap

Begin working on Round 11 (9, 7, 5, 3, 1) for each size and to begin decreasing. For example, the smallest size SKIPS Rounds 1-10 and ONLY works Rounds 11-22. The largest size works ALL rounds.

CHICK FEED
This is a great example of crocheting a tube. Don't be shy; give it a try! Quick gift idea: Crochet this cap for every member of the family in custom colors and patterns.

ADVANCED BEGINNER

ROUND 1 *1 sc in next 10 sc, sc2tog*. Repeat from * to * around—77 sts.

ROUND 2 Work 1 sc in each sc around.

ROUND 3 *1 sc in next 9 sc, sc2tog*. Repeat from * to * around—70 sts.

ROUND 4 Work 1 sc in each sc around.

ROUND 5 *1 sc in next 8 sc, sc2tog*. Repeat from * to * around—63 sts.

ROUND 6 Work 1 sc in each sc around.

ROUND 7 *1 sc in next 7 sc, sc2tog*. Repeat from * to * around—56 sts.

ROUND 8 Work 1 sc in each sc around.

ROUND 9 *1 sc in next 6 sc, sc2tog*. Repeat from * to * around—49 sts.

ROUND 10 Work 1 sc in each sc around.

ROUND 11 *1 sc in next 5 sc, sc2tog*. Repeat from * to * around—42 sts.

ROUND 12 Work 1 sc in each sc around.

ROUND 13 *1 sc in next 4 sc, sc2tog*. Repeat from * to * around—35 sts.

ROUND 14 Work 1 sc in each sc around.

ROUND 15 *1 sc in next 3 sc, sc2tog*. Repeat from * to * around—28 sts.

ROUND 16 Work 1 sc in each sc around.

ROUND 17 *1 sc in next 2 sc, sc2tog*. Repeat from * to * around—21 sts.

ROUND 18 Work 1 sc in each sc around.

ROUND 19 *1 sc in next sc, sc2tog*. Repeat from * to * around—14 sts.

ROUND 20 Work 1 sc in each sc around.

ROUND 21 *Sc2tog*. Repeat form * to * around—7 sts.

ROUND 22 Work 1 sc in next sc, *sc2tog*. Repeat from * to * around—4 sts.

Cut yarn leaving approximately a 6" tail. Weave tail through last 4 sts and tighten. Fasten off and weave in all yarn ends.

71

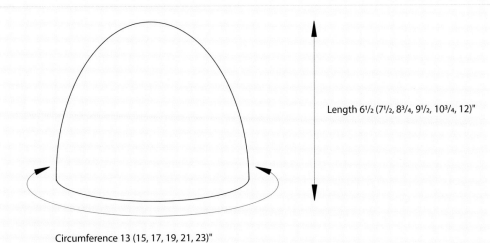

Length 6½ (7½, 8¾, 9½, 10¾, 12)"

Circumference 13 (15, 17, 19, 21, 23)"

smellin'-like-a-rose washcloths

completed measurements
Approximately
$8\frac{1}{2}$" x $8\frac{1}{2}$"

materials
115 yd/105 m worsted weight cotton in pink (A)

115 yd/105 m worsted weight cotton in lime green (B)

115 yd/105 m worsted weight cotton in orange (C)

Size F/5 (3.75 mm) crochet hook

Finishing needle

SAMPLES WERE CROCHETED USING MANOS DEL URUGUAY "COTTON STRIA" (1.75 OZ/50 G, 116 YD/106 M PER HANK; 100% COTTON) IN BUBBLEGUM 207, PISTACHIO 204, AND TANGERINE 206.

abbreviation key

ch	chain
ch-sp	chain-space
lp	loop
sc	single crochet
sk	skip
sl st	slip stitch
st(s)	stitch(es)

gauge
20 sc to 4" using size F/5 (3.75 mm) crochet hook or size needed to obtain gauge

NOTE: SEE LESSON 11, "CHAIN GANG," (PAGE 85) FOR CHAIN-SPACE STITCH HELP.

Washcloth

NOTE: ROUNDS ARE WORKED CONTINUOUSLY; DO NOT TURN AT THE END OF A ROUND.

Using yarn A, ch 2

ROUND 1 Work 5 sc in second ch from hook.

ROUND 2 *Ch 5, work 1 sc in next sc*. Repeat from * to * another 4 times.

ROUND 3 Work 1 sl st in each of next 3 chs. *Ch 5 and work 1 sc in next ch-5 lp*. Repeat from * to * another 4 times.

ROUND 4 Change to yarn B. *Ch 4, work 2 sc in next ch-5 sp, 1 sc in next sc*. Repeat from * to * another 4 times.

CHICK FEED
The natural slubs in the nubbed cotton we used for making these washcloths are ideal for scrubbing. The updated design makes it pretty enough to show off in your kitchen or powder room. P.S. Don't forget to wash behind the ears!

ADVANCED BEGINNER

ROUND 5 *Ch 4, work 2 sc in next ch-4 sp, 1 sc in each of next 2 sc*. Repeat from * to * another 4 times.

ROUND 6 *Ch 4, work 2 sc in next ch-4 sp, 1 sc in each of next 3 sc, sk next sc*. Repeat from * to * another 4 times.

ROUND 7 *Ch 4, work 2 sc in next ch-4 sp, 1 sc in each of next 4 sc, sk next sc*. Repeat from * to * another 4 times.

ROUND 8 *Ch 4, work 2 sc in next ch-4 sp, 1 sc in each of next 5 sc, sk next sc*. Repeat from * to * another 4 times.

ROUND 9 *Ch 4, work 2 sc in next ch-4 sp, 1 sc in each of next 6 sc, sk next sc*. Repeat from * to * another 4 times.

ROUND 10 *Ch 4, work 2 sc in next ch-4 sp, 1 sc in each of next 7 sc, sk next sc*. Repeat from * to * another 4 times.

ROUND 11 *Ch 4, work 2 sc in next ch-4 sp, 1 sc in each of next 8 sc, sk next sc*. Repeat from * to * another 4 times.

ROUND 12 *Ch 4, work 2 sc in next ch-4 sp, 1 sc in each of next 9 sc, sk next sc*. Repeat from * to * another 4 times.

ROUND 13 *Ch 4, work 2 sc in next ch-4 sp, 1 sc in each of next 10 sc, sk next sc*. Repeat from * to * another 4 times.

ROUND 14 *Ch 4, work 2 sc in next ch-4 sp, 1 sc in each of next 11 sc, sk next sc*. Repeat from * to * another 4 times.

ROUND 15 *Ch 4, work 2 sc in next ch-4 sp, 1 sc in each of next 12 sc, sk next sc*. Repeat from * to * another 4 times.

ROUND 16 *Ch 4, work 2 sc in next ch-4 sp, 1 sc in each of next 13 sc, sk next sc*. Repeat from * to * another 4 times.

ROUND 17 *Ch 4, work 2 sc in next ch-4 sp, 1 sc in each of next 14 sc, sk next sc*. Repeat from * to * another 4 times.

ROUND 18 *Ch 4, work 2 sc in next ch-4 sp, 1 sc in each of next 15 sc, sk next sc*. Repeat from * to * another 4 times.

ROUND 19 *Ch 4, work 2 sc in next ch-4 sp, 1 sc in each of next 16 sc, sk next sc*. Repeat from * to * another 4 times.

ROUND 20 *Ch 4, work 2 sc in next ch-4 sp, 1 sc in each of next 17 sc, sk next sc*. Repeat from * to * another 4 times.

ROUND 21 *Ch 4, work 2 sc in next ch-4 sp, 1 sc in each of next 18 sc, sk next sc*. Repeat from * to * another 4 times.

ROUND 22 *Ch 4, work 2 sc in next ch-4 sp, 1 sc in each of next 19 sc, sk next sc*. Repeat from * to * another 4 times.

ROUND 23 *Ch 4, work 2 sc in next ch-4 sp, 1 sc in each of next 20 sc, sk next sc*. Repeat from * to * another 4 times.

ROUND 24 *Ch 4, work 2 sc in next ch-4 sp, 1 sc in each of next 21 sc, sk next sc*. Repeat from * to * another 4 times.

ROUND 25 *Ch 4, work 2 sc in next ch-4 sp, 1 sc in each of next 22 sc, sk next sc*. Repeat from * to * another 4 times. Fasten off and weave in all yarn ends.

Make another washcloth using yarn B then C.

Make another washcloth using yarn C then A.

CHEEP TRICKS
Make sure you leave at least a 4-6" tail when ending or beginning a new ball of yarn. You will need to have a long enough tail to weave in later.

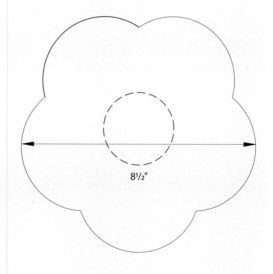

8¹/₂"

AND YOU CALL YOURSELF A SHRINK!

Cool Facts About Felting

Have you ever shrunk a wool sweater by accident? Well, felting is the process of purposely shrinking wool using hot or warm water and agitation. This irreversible process causes the wool hairs to tangle and bind together to form a very thick, durable fabric. Does the type of yarn you select matter? Yes! You need to choose yarn that is 100% wool, suitable for felting. Some merino wools have been treated so they will not felt. Most wool blends also will not felt. Your local yarn shop can help you select wools that are appropriate for this process.

TO FELT A PROJECT YOU WILL NEED:

- A washing machine with good agitation.
- A zippered pillow protector (a lingerie bag is not suitable to protect your washer from excess lint and fiber).
- An old pair of jeans or khakis.
- A few large towels.

STEP-BY-STEP FELTING INSTRUCTIONS

1. Be prepared to be near your washing machine during the felting process. Set washer to the smallest load and hottest water settings. Add a small amount of laundry soap. Place item to be felted inside pillow protector and place in washing machine. Add a pair of jeans or khakis to help with the agitation process.
2. Check washer after 5 minutes; the wool will absorb the water and actually seem to get looser.
3. Check washer after 8-10 minutes. You should notice the stitches becoming "fuzzier" and beginning to blur together.

4. Check again every 3-5 minutes. Do NOT allow machine to go through the rinse or spin cycles. When the felting item appears to be the correct size (you should no longer be able to see the stitches, and the fabric will feel very thick), remove from washer and hand rinse in cold water.

5. Gently squeeze out excess water (do not wring). Wrap the item in towels to remove as much water as possible. Do NOT put your project in the dryer.

6. After you have felted a project and you remove it from the washing machine, think of it as a ball of clay. You may need to stretch and shape it a bit to achieve just the right look. Don't be afraid to really give it a tug or pull—it is quite strong. When felting tote bags, we always try to find an empty box to use as a mold. Allow to air-dry overnight.

CHEEP TRICKS

You'll need to experiment to get the look you want. Every washing machine felts differently and each item you felt may require a different amount of felting time . . . felting is an art, not a science!

DON'T MISS A CHANCE TO GET FELTED!

There are several projects in this book in which you can test out your new felting skills, following these instructions. Be sure to try them all! In addition to the Laguna Felted Bag and the Large Felted Christmas Stocking on the following pages, check these out:

- Chicks' Slit-Top Felted Bag, page 33
- Laguna Felted Crochet Hook Case, page 35
- Chicks' Felted Zebra Slippers, page 127
- Pocket Full of Posies Felted Purse, page 139

laguna felted bag

SAMPLE WAS CROCHETED USING MANOS DEL URUGUAY WOOL (3.5 OZ/100 G, 138 YD/126 M PER HANK; 100% PURE WOOL) PURPLE, AQUA BLUE, AND LIME GREEN.

completed measurements

Approximately 12" x 8" x 5" after felting

materials

120 yd/110 m light chunky weight wool for felting in aqua blue (A)

220 yd/201 m light chunky weight wool for felting in purple (B)

120 yd/110 m light chunky weight wool for felting in lime green (C)

Size N/15 (10.0 mm) crochet hook

Finishing needle

abbreviation key

ch   chain

sc   single crochet

sk   skip

gauge

8 sts and 11 rows to 4" over sc on size N/15 (10.0 mm hook) or size needed to obtain gauge

Bag Bottom

Using yarn A, ch 41

ROW 1   Work 1 sc in second ch from hook and in each ch across—40 sc.

ROW 2   Ch 1 and turn. 1 sc in each sc across.

Repeat Row 2 another 18 times. You should have 20 rows total. Change to yarn B and begin Bag Sides.

Bag Sides

NOTE: ROUNDS ARE WORKED CONTINUOUSLY. DO NOT JOIN OR TURN. PLACE MARKER AT BEGINNING OF EACH ROUND.

ROUND 1   Pick up and work evenly around outside edges of bottom as follows: Work 16 sc along short side, 40 sc along long side, 16 sc long next side, 40 sc along remaining side—112 sc total.

CHICK FEED

Not only is this tote a fabulous carryall for your crochet projects, it also coordinates with the Laguna Crochet Hook Case on page 35. Crocheted on a large hook, it works up relatively fast. You will crochet the bottom first, then work around the outside edges, and then simply around and around until you reach the top opening.

BEGINNER

ROUNDS 2-6   1 sc in each sc around.

ROUND 7   *Work 1 sc in next 12 sc, dec 1 sc over next 2 sc*. Repeat from * to * around—104 sc.

ROUNDS 8-13   1 sc in each sc around.

ROUND 14   *Work 1 sc in next 11 sc, dec 1 sc over next 2 sc*. Repeat from * to * around—96 sc.

ROUNDS 15-20   1 sc in each sc around.

ROUND 21   *Work 1 sc in next 10 sc, dec 1 sc over next 2 sc*. Repeat from *to * around—88 sc.

ROUNDS 22-27   1 sc in each sc around.

ROUND 28   *Work 1 sc in next 9 sc, dec 1 sc over next 2 sc*. Repeat from * to * around—80 sc.

ROUNDS 29-33   1 sc in each sc around.

ROUND 34   Change to yarn A, work 1 sc in next 8 sc, dec 1 sc over next 2 sc*. *Repeat from * to * around—72 sc.

ROUND 35   Work 1 row of sc in each sc around.

Fasten off and weave in all yarn ends.

Handles (make 2)
Using yarn C, ch 41

ROW 1   Work 1 sc in second ch from hook and in each ch across—40 sc.

ROW 2   Ch 1 and turn. Work 1 sc in each sc across.

Repeat Row 2 another 2 times. You should have 4 rows total.

Finishing
See felting instructions on page 75. Whipstich the handle to the bag after felting while the bag and handles are still damp and use a sharp needle. If you wait until the pieces are dry it will be much more difficult to sew them together.

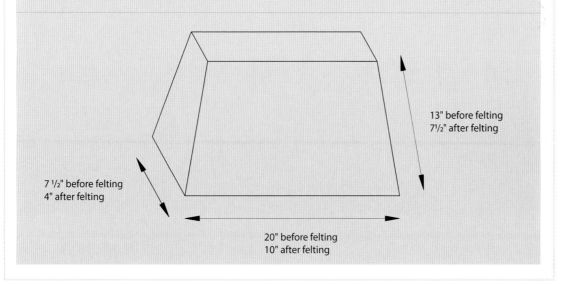

13" before felting
7½" after felting

7 ½" before felting
4" after felting

20" before felting
10" after felting

| large felted christmas stocking |

completed measurements

Approximately 20" around at cuff x 23" long before felting

Approximately 13" around at cuff x 18" long after felting

materials

130 yd/119 m light chunky weight wool for felting, in olive (A)

130 yd/119 m light chunky weight wool for felting in green (B)

350 yd/320 m light chunky weight wool for felting in red (C)

Size L/11 (8.0 mm crochet hook)

Finishing needle

STOCKING IN PHOTOGRAPH WAS CROCHETED USING MANOS DEL URUGUAY WOOL (3.5 OZ/100 G, 138 YD/116 M PER HANK; 100% PURE WOOL) IN POPPY, OLIVE, AND CITRIC.

abbreviation key

beg	beginning
ch	chain
sc	single crochet
sc2tog	single crochet two stitches together
sk	skip
sl st	slip stitch
st(s)	stitch(es)

gauge

11 sts and 14 rows to 4" over sc on size L/11 (8.0 mm) hook or size needed to obtain gauge

Top Cuff

Using yarn A, ch 56

ROUND 1   Join with sl st to beg ch. Ch 1 and turn. Work 1 sc in each ch around.

ROUND 2   Join with sl st to beg sc. Ch 1 and turn. Work 1 sc in each sc around.

ROUND 3   Change to yarn B and join with sl st to beg sc. Ch 1 and turn. Work 1 sc in each sc around.

ROUND 4   Join with sl st to beg sc. Ch 1 and turn. Work 1 sc in each sc around.

ROUND 5   Change to yarn A and join with sl st to beg sc. Ch 1 and turn. Work 1 sc in each sc around.

ROUND 6   Join with sl st to beg sc. Ch 1 and turn. Work 1 sc in each sc around.

ROUND 7   Change to yarn B and join with sl st to beg sc. Ch 1 and turn. Work 1 sc in each sc around.

ROUND 8   Join with sl st to beg sc. Ch 1 and turn. Work 1 sc in each sc around.

Repeat Rounds 5-8 1 more time.

ADVANCED BEGINNER

CHICK FEED
Any child will be excited to hang this oversized stocking on the mantel on Christmas Eve. Nancy originally crocheted this for her daughter, who was thrilled, since Santa needed quite a large pile of goodies to fill it all the way to the top. This fun-to-make stocking is single crocheted in the round and then felted.

Leg

ROUND 1 Change to yarn C and join with sl st to beg sc. Ch 1 and turn. Work 1 sc in each sc in BACK LOOPS only.

ROUND 2 Join with sl st to beg sc. Ch 1 and turn. Work 1 sc in each sc around.

Repeat Round 2 another 34 times. You should have 48 rounds total from the beginning.

Heel

ROW 1 Change to yarn B and join with sl st to beg sc. Ch 1 and turn. Work 1 sc in each of next 28 sc.

ROW 2 Ch 1 and turn. Work 1 sc in each sc across — 28 sc.

ROW 3 Change to yarn A. Ch 1 and turn. Work 1 sc in each sc across.

ROW 4 Ch 1 and turn. Work 1 sc in each sc across.

ROW 5 Change to yarn B. Ch 1 and turn. Work 1 sc in each sc across.

ROW 6 Ch 1 and turn. Work 1 sc in each sc across.

ROW 7 Change to yarn A. Ch 1 and turn. Work 1 sc in each sc across.

ROW 8 Ch 1 and turn. Work 1 sc in each sc across.

Repeat Rows 5-8 another 4 times. You should have 24 rows total.

BEGIN HEEL SHAPING

ROW 1 Change to yarn B. Ch 1 and turn. Work 1 sc in each of next 16 sc, sc2tog, 1 sc in next sc.

ROW 2 Ch 1 and turn. 1 sc in next 6 sc. Sc2tog working in remaining st in row and next st of previous row. Work 1 sc in next st of previous row.

ROW 3 Change to yarn A. Ch 1 and turn. 1 sc in next 7 sc. Sc2tog working in remaining st in row and next st of previous row. Work 1 sc in next st of previous row.

ROW 4 Ch 1 and turn. 1 sc in next 8 sc. Sc2tog working in remaining st in row and next st of previous row. Work 1 sc in next st of previous row.

ROW 5 Change to yarn B. Ch 1 and turn. 1 sc in next 9 sc. Sc2tog working in remaining st in row and next st of previous row. Work 1 sc in next st of previous row.

ROW 6 Ch 1 and turn. 1 sc in next 10 sc. Sc2tog working in remaining st in row and next st of previous row. Work 1 sc in next st of previous row.

ROW 7 Change to yarn A. Ch 1 and turn. 1 sc in next 11 sc. Sc2tog working in remaining st in row and next st of previous row. Work 1 sc in next st of previous row.

ROW 8 Ch 1 and turn. 1 sc in next 12 sc. Sc2tog working in remaining st in row and next st of previous row. Work 1 sc in next st of previous row.

ROW 9 Change to yarn B. Ch 1 and turn. 1 sc in next 13 sc. Sc2tog working in remaining st in row and next st of previous row. Work 1 sc in next st of previous row.

ROW 10 Ch 1 and turn. 1 sc in next 14 sc. Sc2tog working in remaining st in row and next st of previous row. Work 1 sc in next st of previous row.

ROW 11 Change to yarn A. Ch 1 and turn. 1 sc in next 15 sc. Sc2tog working in remaining st in row and next st of previous row.

ROW 12 Ch 1 and turn. 1 sc in next 15 sc. Sc2tog.

WORK HEEL GUSSET

Change to yarn C. Ch 1 and turn. Work 1 sc in next 16 sts along heel flap. Evenly work 15 sc along side of heel. Place marker. Work 1 sc in each of the 28 sts along instep. Place marker. Evenly work 15 sc along remaining side heel. You should have 74 sts total.

ROUND 1 Join with sl st to first sc in round. Ch 1 and turn. Work 1 sc in each sc around to first marker, sc2tog. Work 1 sc in each sc around to next marker, sc2tog. Work 1 sc in each sc to end of round—72 sts.

Repeat Round 1 another 8 times until 56 sts remain.

Continue working rounds in sc until foot measures 8½″.

SHAPE TOE

ROUND 1 Change to yarn B. Join with sl st to first sc in round. Ch 1 and turn. Work 1 sc in each of next 26 sc, sc2tog. Work 1 sc in each of next 26 sc, sc2tog.

ROUND 2 Join with sl st to first sc in round. Ch 1 and turn. Work 1 sc in each of next 25 sc, sc2tog. Work 1 sc in each of next 25 sc, sc2tog.

ROUND 3 Change to yarn A. Join with sl st to first sc in round. Ch 1 and turn. Work 1 sc in each of next 24 sc, sc2tog. Work 1 sc in each of next 24 sc, sc2tog.

ROUND 4 Join with sl st to first sc in round. Ch 1 and turn. Work 1 sc in each of next 23 sc, sc2tog. Work 1 sc in each of next 23 sc, sc2tog.

ROUND 5 Change to yarn B. Join with sl st to first sc in round. Ch 1 and turn. Work 1 sc in each of next 22 sc, sc2tog. Work 1 sc in each of next 22 sc, sc2tog.

ROUND 6 Join with sl st to first sc in round. Ch 1 and turn. Work 1 sc in each of next 21 sc, sc2tog. Work 1 sc in each of next 21 sc, sc2tog.

ROUND 7 Change to yarn A. Join with sl st to first sc in round. Ch 1 and turn. Work 1 sc in each of next 20 sc, sc2tog. Work 1 sc in each of next 20 sc, sc2tog.

ROUND 8 Join with sl st to first sc in round. Ch 1 and turn. Work 1 sc in each of next 19 sc, sc2tog. Work 1 sc in each of next 19 sc, sc2tog.

ROUND 9 Change to yarn B. Join with sl st to first sc in round. Ch 1 and turn. Work 1 sc in each of next 18 sc, sc2tog. Work 1 sc in each of next 18 sc, sc2tog.

ROUND 10 Join with sl st to first sc in round. Ch 1 and turn. Work 1 sc in each of next 17 sc, sc2tog. Work 1 sc in each of next 17 sc, sc2tog.

ROUND 11 Change to yarn A. Join with sl st to first sc in round. Ch 1 and turn. Work 1 sc in each of next 16 sc, sc2tog. Work 1 sc in each of next 16 sc, sc2tog.

ROUND 12 Join with sl st to first sc in round. Ch 1 and turn. Work 1 sc in each of next 15 sc, sc2tog. Work 1 sc in each of next 15 sc, sc2tog.

ROUND 13 Change to yarn B. Join with sl st to first sc in round. Ch 1 and turn. Work 1 sc in each of next 14 sc, sc2tog. Work 1 sc in each of next 14 sc, sc2tog.

Finish off, leaving a long tail (approximately 18"). Join top and bottom of toe and sew seam using tail. Fasten off and weave in all yarn ends.

TOP LOOP

Using yarn A, ch 11

Beg in second ch from hook, work 1 sc in each sc across. Fasten off.

Use horizontal mattress stitch to sew both ends to top of cuff to make a loop. Weave in all yarn ends.

Follow felting instructions at beginning of this lesson.

84

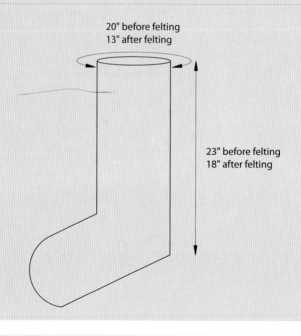

20" before felting
13" after felting

23" before felting
18" after felting

Stitch Variation

So far you have learned the five basic stitches of crochet: slip stitch, single crochet, half double crochet, double crochet, and treble crochet. All other stitches are simply a combination or variation of these five stitches. There are hundreds of stitch variations available. You will learn a few of the most popular combinations in the upcoming lessons. If you really enjoy working the stitch variations, it would be wise to invest in a stitch dictionary at your local bookstore or yarn shop.

Chain-Space (ch-sp)

You don't always need to put your hook into a stitch to form the next stitch. Let's say on a previously worked row you were required to make holes by crocheting one or more chains. The space (or hole) that was made in the previous row is now called a chain-space in the current row. Instead of inserting your hook into the next stitch, you will insert your hook into the chain-space. For example, sometimes a pattern will state: "Row 1: 1 dc, ch 2, 1 dc. Row 2: 1 dc, 3 dc in ch-2 sp, 1 dc." In the case of the chain-2 space, you will be working 3 double crochet stitches in the hole made when you chained 2 in the middle of the previous row.

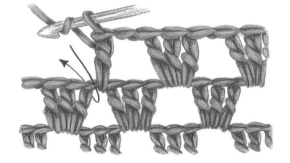

our esprit pullover

sizes

Small 4-6 (Medium 8-10, Large 12-14)

Fits bust sizes: 30 (32-34, 36-38, 40-42)"

completed chest measurements

35 (40, 44, 47)"

NOTE: THIS GARMENT HAS A RELAXED, BOXY FIT.

materials

560 (640, 720, 800) yd/512 (858, 658, 732) m chunky weight yarn in green

Size K/10.5 (6.5 mm) crochet hook

Finishing needle

SAMPLE WAS CROCHETED USING GGH/MUENCH YARN "ESPRIT" (1.75 OZ/50 G, 80 YD/73 M PER BALL; 100% NYLON) IN OLIVE.

abbreviation key

beg	beginning
ch	chain
ch-3 sp	chain-three space
dc	double crochet
sk	skip
t-ch	turning chain

gauge

12 sts to 4" over dc on K/10.5 (6.5mm) hook or size needed to obtain gauge

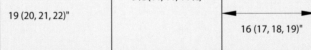

4 (4, 5½, 6)"

9½ (11, 11, 11½)"

19 (20, 21, 22)"

16 (17, 18, 19)"

17½ (20, 22, 23½)"

CHICK FEED

Not only did Nancy love the feel of this yarn, but "Esprit" was also the name of her favorite clothing brand in high school (my, aren't we dating ourselves!). Taking inspiration from Esprit, she designed this sweater with an open, lighthearted, youthful feel. The Our Esprit Pullover has a relaxed, casual fit and no shaping.

ADVANCED BEGINNER

Front/Back (make 2)

Ch 75 (81, 87, 93) very loosely

ROW 1 Work 1 dc in fourth ch from hook, 1 dc in next ch. *Ch 3, sk next 3 chs, work 1 dc in each of next 3 chs*. Repeat from * to * across to last 4 chs. Ch 3, sk next 3 chs, work 1 dc in last ch.

ROW 2 Ch 3 and turn. Sk first dc, work 2 dc in next ch-3 sp. *Ch 3, sk next 3 dc, 3 dc in next ch-3 sp*. Repeat from * to * across to last 2 dc. Ch 3, sk next 2 dc, work 1 dc in t-ch.

Repeat Row 2 until panel measures approximately 19 (20, 21, 22)" from the beg.

Sleeves (make 2)

Ch 39 (39, 45, 45) very loosely

ROW 1 Work 1 dc in fourth ch from hook, 1 dc in next ch. *Ch 3, sk next chs, work 1 dc in each of next 3 chs*. Repeat from * to * across to last 4 chs. Ch 3, sk next 3 chs, work 1 dc in last ch.

ROW 2 Ch 3 and turn. Sk first dc, work 2 dc in next ch-3 sp. *Ch 3, sk next 3 dc, 3 dc in next ch-3 sp*. Repeat from * to * across to last 2 dc. Ch 3, sk next 2 dc, work 1 dc in t-ch.

Repeat Row 2 until panel measures approximately 16 (17, 18, 19)" from the beg.

Finishing

Note before finishing: Refer to Lesson 19, "Get It Together," (page 148) for instructions on various finishing techniques.

Beg at sleeve edge, sew front to back along first 4 (4, 5½, 6)" of shoulder seams.

Sew sleeve top to armhole, easing to fit. Sew side and sleeve seams. Weave in all loose ends.

The best stitch for sewing these seams is whipstitch.

Cobble Stitch (a.k.a. Griddle Stitch, Up-and-Down Stitch)

Most of the projects we have worked on so far have been comprised of just one type of stitch, such as all single crochet or all double crochet. The cobble stitch is done by alternating single crochet and double crochet, and it ends up looking much like a checkerboard, with its red and black blocks alternating rows. The result is a bumpy yet very pretty stitch. In this lesson we introduce the cobble stitch with the easy-to-crochet Artisan Belt, a project that can be easily adapted into a scarf or shawl by making it a bit wider; just remember to make your foundation chain with an odd number of stitches.

The two sweater projects that follow this lesson are amazingly fast to make! Here's why: Since you have to pay closer attention to what you are doing (more so than with straight single crochet or double crochet), the stitch does not get boring. And for better drape, we often "open up" this stitch by using a larger hook. Fast and fun...what more could you ask for?

artisan belt

completed measurements

For tie belt: measure your waist and add 6"

For buckle belt: measure your waist and add 2"

Don't make it too long. These belts stretch a lot with wear.

materials

100 yd/91 m worsted weight yarn in any fiber

Size J/10 (6.0 mm) crochet hook

Finishing needle

Belt buckle (optional)

SAMPLE WAS CROCHETED USING JUDY & CO. "CORDE" (3.5 OZ/100 G, 100 YD/91 M PER HANK; 100% RAYON WITH A COTTON CORE) IN HARVEST.

abbreviation key

ch	chain
dc	double crochet
sc	single crochet
st(s)	stitch(es)

gauge

5 sts to 1" over Cobble Stitch on size J/10 (6.0 mm) hook or size needed to obtain gauge

Cobble Stitch

Work 1 sc in next dc, 1 dc in next sc.

BELT

Ch 11

ROW 1 Work 1 sc in second ch from hook, 1 dc in next ch, *1 sc in next ch, 1 dc in next ch. Repeat from * to * across—10 sts.

ROW 2 Ch 1 and turn. *Work 1 sc in next dc. Work 1 dc in next sc*. Repeat from * to * across.

Repeat Row 2 until panel measures desired length.

Fasten off and weave in all yarn ends.

OPTIONAL BUCKLE

Slip one end of belt through buckle, fold over, and sew into place.

90

2"

Work to desired length

CHICK FEED
Put the Artisan Belt on your "Quick Gifts to Crochet in a Pinch" list! Just about any yarn will make an interesting belt. It can be a tie or buckle closure belt. You can add fringe or not. Use your yarn stash, be an artist, and create something truly unique.

BEGINNER

the no-sweat hoodie

sizes
Small (Medium, Large, X-Large)

completed chest measurements
34 (36, 38, 40)"

materials
550 (660, 660, 770) yd/ 503 (604, 604, 704) m chunky weight wool or wool blend yarn in gray

Size P/16 (11.5 mm) crochet hook

Finishing needle

GARMENT IN PHOTOGRAPH WAS CROCHETED USING PLYMOUTH "BABY ALPACA GRANDE" (3.5 OZ/100 G, 110 YD/100 M PER HANK; 100% BABY ALPACA) IN GRAY #401.

abbreviation key
beg	beginning
ch	chain
dc	double crochet
dec 1	decrease one stitch
sc	single crochet
sk	skip
st(s)	stitch(es)

gauge
8 sts and 7 rows to 4" over Cobble Stitch on size P/16 (11.5 mm) hook or size needed to obtain gauge

ADVANCED BEGINNER

Cobble Stitch

Work 1 sc in next dc, 1 dc in next sc.

BACK

Ch 37 (39, 41, 43)

ROW 1   Work 1 sc in second ch from hook, 1 dc in next ch, *1 sc in next ch, 1 dc in next ch*. Repeat from * to * across—36 (38, 40, 42) sts.

ROW 2   Ch 1 and turn. *Work 1 sc in next dc, 1 dc in next sc*. Repeat from * to * across.

Repeat Row 2 another 20 (20, 20, 22) times. You should have 22 (22, 22, 24) rows total.

Continuing in Cobble St, begin armhole shaping as follows: Sk last 1 (2, 2, 2) sts at end of next 2 rows. Dec 1 st at armhole ends of every 2nd row 4 (5, 4, 3) times, then dec 1 st at armhole ends of every row 6 (4, 6, 8) times. You should have 38 (38, 38, 40) rows total with 14 (16, 16, 17) sts remaining. Fasten off.

Front

Ch 37 (39, 41, 43)

ROW 1   Work 1 sc in second ch from hook, 1 dc in next ch, *1 sc in next ch, 1 dc in next ch*. Repeat from * to * across—36 (38, 40, 42) sts.

ROW 2   Ch 1 and turn. *Work 1 sc in next dc, 1 dc in next sc*. Repeat from * to * across.

Repeat Row 2 another 20 (20, 20, 22) times. You should have 22 (22, 22, 24) rows total.

Continuing in Cobble St, begin armhole shaping as follows: Sk last 1 (2, 2, 2) sts at end of the next 2 rows. Dec 1 st at armhole ends of every 2nd row 4 (5, 4, 3) times, then dec 1 st at armhole ends of every row 6 (4, 6, 8) times. Continue until you have completed the first 10 rows of armhole shaping. You should have 26 (26, 28, 29) sts remaining. Then shape neckline as follows, continuing armhole shaping AT THE SAME TIME.

SHAPE NECK

Work 1 st in each of first 10 (10, 11, 12) sts. Skip next 6 (6, 6, 5) sts. Attach another ball of yarn and work 1 st in each of remaining 10 (10, 11, 12) sts. Continue working in Cobble St and work both sides AT THE SAME TIME. Dec 1 st at neck edge of every row 2 (3, 3, 4) times, until 4 (3, 3, 2) sts remain. Work even at neck edge, continuing armhole decreases to last 2 sts. Fasten off.

Sleeves (make 2)

Ch 19 (19, 19, 21)

ROW 1 Work 1 sc in second ch from hook, 1 dc in next ch, *1 sc in next ch, 1 dc in next ch*. Repeat from * to * across–18 (18, 18, 20) sts.

ROW 2 Ch 1 and turn. *Work 1 sc in next dc, 1 dc in next sc*. Repeat from * to * across.

Continuing in Cobble St, work sleeve shaping as follows:

Increase 1 st at each end of every 7th (7th, 6th, 6th) row 1 (1, 4, 4) times, then every 8th (8th, 0, 0) row to 2 (2, 0, 0) to 24 (24, 26, 28) sts. You should have 23 (23, 24, 24) rows total.

Work even for another 7 (7, 6, 6) rows. You should have 30 rows total.

Continuing in Cobble St, work raglan shaping as follows: Sk last 1 (2, 2, 2) sts of next 2 rows. Dec 1 st at each end of every 2nd row 4 (5, 4, 3) times, then dec 1 st at each end of every row 6 (4, 6, 8) times. Fasten off.

Hood

Loosely ch 55 (55, 57, 57)

ROW 1 Work 1 sc in second ch from hook, 1 dc in next ch, *1 sc in next ch, 1 dc in next ch*. Repeat from * to * across – 54 (54, 56, 56) sts.

ROW 2 Ch 1 and turn. *Work 1 sc in next dc, 1 dc in next sc*. Repeat from * to * across.

Continuing in Cobble St work hood shaping as follows:
Dec 1 st at each end of next row, then every following row 6 times until 40 (40, 42, 42) sts remain. Continue working until you have 16 rows from the beg. Fasten off.

Finishing

Note before finishing: Refer to Lesson 19, "Get It Together," (page 148) for instructions on various finishing techniques.

Using the mattress stitch, sew sleeves to front and back, along raglan armhole seams. Then sew sleeve top to armhole, easing to fit. Next sew side and sleeve seams.

Then sew back seam of hood.

Place hood around neckline and, using a single crochet seam, sew bottom of hood to neckline. Weave in all yarn ends.

CHICK FEED
The No-Sweat Hoodie will quickly become one of your favorite sweaters to wear.
We cut it a little loose and boxy to fit more like a comfortable old sweatshirt.
It's crocheted on a big hook, not only to make it a fast project, but also to allow
for the yarn to drape gently. This makes for a cozier feel and all but guarantees this
sweater will soon become one of your favorites!

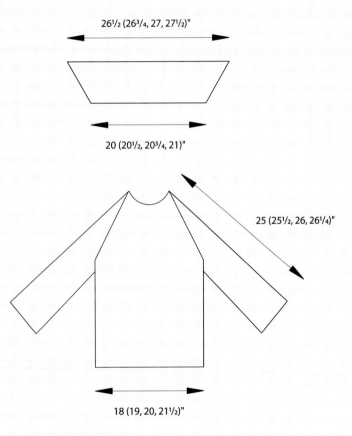

26½ (26¾, 27, 27½)"

20 (20½, 20¾, 21)"

25 (25½, 26, 26¼)"

18 (19, 20, 21½)"

big 'n' rich pullover

sizes

Small (Medium, Large, X-Large)

completed chest measurements

32 (36, 38, 40)"

materials

580 (660, 720, 840) yd/ 530, 603, 768 m super chunky weight wool or wool blend yarn in charcoal

Size Q (16.0 mm) crochet hook

Size P (11.5 mm) crochet hook for finishing

Finishing needle

SAMPLE WAS CROCHETED USING COLINETTE "POINT 5" (3.5 OZ/ 100 G, 58 YD/53 M PER HANK; 100% PURE WOOL) IN BRIGHT CHARCOAL.

abbreviation key

beg	beginning
ch	chain
dc	double crochet
dec 1	decrease one stitch
sc	single crochet
st	stitch

gauge

5½ sts and 5½ rows to 4" over Cobble Stitch using Size P (11.5 mm) hook or size needed to obtain gauge

Cobble Stitch

Work 1 sc in next dc, 1 dc in next sc.

Back

Using larger hook, ch 25 (27, 29, 31)

ROW 1   Work 1 sc in 2nd ch from hook, work 1 dc in next ch. *1 sc in next ch, 1 dc in next ch*. Repeat from * to * across–24 (26, 28, 30) sts.

ROW 2   Ch 1 and turn. Working in Cobble St, work 1 sc in next dc, 1 dc in next sc.

Repeat Row 2 another 12 (14, 14, 16) rows.

Begin armhole shaping as follows:
Skip 1 st at end of next 2 rows.

Continuing in Cobble St, dec 1 st at each end of every other row 1 (2, 3, 3) times. You should have 20 (20, 20, 22) sts.

CHICK FEED
Picture this ski weekend getaway: You just had a fabulous day on the slopes. You've come in from the cold and are ready to slip into something more comfortable. Your Big 'n' Rich Pullover will keep you snuggly warm while you're curled up in front of a roaring fire with a mug of steaming hot chocolate.

ADVANCED BEGINNER

Continue in Cobble St until you have 28 (30, 30, 32) rows from the beg. Fasten off.

Front

Using larger hook, ch 25 (27, 29, 31)

ROW 1 Work 1 sc in 2nd ch from hook, work 1 dc in next ch. *1 sc in next ch, 1 dc in next ch*. Repeat from * to * across—24 (26, 28, 30) sts.

ROW 2 Ch 1 and turn. Working in Cobble St, work 1 sc in next dc, 1 dc in next sc.

Repeat Row 2 another 12 (14, 14, 16) rows.

Begin armhole shaping as follows and AT THE SAME TIME work neck shaping:

Sk 1 st at end of next 2 rows.

Continuing in Cobble St, dec 1 st at each end of every other row 1 (2, 3, 3) times.

NECK SHAPE

Work both sides AT THE SAME TIME. Work across first 11 (12, 13, 14) sts. Attach another ball of yarn and work across remaining 11 (12, 13, 14) sts. Dec 1 st at neck edge of next row, then every 3rd row 3 times until 6 (6, 6, 7) sts remain. Fasten off.

SLEEVES (MAKE 2)

Using larger hook, ch 13

ROW 1 Work 1 sc in 2nd ch from hook, work 1 dc in next ch. *1 sc in next ch, 1 dc in next ch*. Repeat from * to * across—12 sts.

ROW 2 Ch 1 and turn. Working in Cobble St, work 1 sc in next dc, 1 dc in next sc.

ROWS 3-5 Repeat Row 2.

Continuing in Cobble St, begin sleeve shaping as follows: Increase 1 st at each end of this row and every 6th row 2 times to 18 sts—you should have 18 rows total from the beg.

Work evenly for 2 more rows to 20 rows.

SHAPE CAP

Dec 1 st at each end of next row, then dec 1 st at each end of every other row 4 times.

FINAL ROW Dec 1 st at each end of row. Fasten off.

Finishing

Note before finishing: Refer to Lesson 19, "Get It Together," (page 148) for instructions on various finishing techniques.

Using horizontal mattress stitch, sew front to back along shoulder seams.

Using mattress stitch, sew sleeve top to armhole, easing to fit. Then sew side and sleeve seams.

Using smaller hook, work 2 rows sc around neckline edge.

Fasten off and weave in all yarn ends.

25 (25¼, 25½, 25)"

9 (10, 10, 12)"

17½ (19, 20½, 22)"

DON'T GET YOUR STITCHES IN A BUNCH

Cluster Stitch

A cluster stitch simply means working more than one stitch into a space to form, well, a cluster. It gives the appearance of a single stitch. This gives interesting shape and texture to your crocheting since, instead of working one stitch in each stitch evenly—as you have been doing thus far—you will be making several stitches in one stitch and then skipping stitches. There are many variations to a cluster stitch, including popcorn and shell stitch, covered in later lessons. As you progress with your crocheting, it will serve you well to pick up one of the many stitch guides available to expand your skills and knowledge. The various cluster stitches really keep your crocheting fun and interesting.

Here is a sample square for you to see how a cluster stitch may be written. Give it a try with some sample yarn.

Chain 21

ROW 1 Work 2 dc in third ch from hook, *sk next 2 chs, work 3 dc in next ch*. Repeat from * to * across to last 3 chs. Sk next 2 chs, work 1 dc in last ch.

ROW 2 Ch 2 and turn. Work 3 dc in sp between t-ch and first 3-dc cluster. *Work 3 dc bet next two 3-dc clusters*. Repeat from * to * across. Work 1 dc in t-ch.

Repeat Row 2 until panel measures approximately 5" from the beginning. Fasten off and weave in all yarn ends.

| holey cowl pullover |

sizes
Small (Medium, Large)

completed chest measurements
36 (38, 40, 42)"

materials
780 (940, 1,020, 1,170) yd/ 713 (860, 932, 1,070) m light bulky weight wool or wool blend bouclé in periwinkle

Size L/11 (8.0 mm) crochet hook

Size N/15 (10.0 mm) crochet hook for collar

Finishing needle

SAMPLE WAS CROCHETED USING ADRIENNE VITTADINI "PALOMA" (1.75 OZ/50 G, 78 YD/71 M PER BALL; 83% BABY ALPACA, 14% WOOL, 3% NYLON) IN PERIWINKLE.

abbreviation key
beg	beginning
ch(s)	chain(s)
dc	double crochet
sk	skip
sl st	slip stitch
sp	space
t-ch	turning chain

gauge
3 clusters over 4" using size L/11 (8.0 mm) hook or size needed to obtain gauge

---

CHEEP TRICKS
In the gauge above we instruct you to check your gauge over a number of clusters rather than individual stitches. Patterns are occasionally written this way, so we felt it important to include one. Our trick for checking gauge in this situation is to start working on one of the sleeves FIRST. After you've worked 4" long, check your gauge. It's a little wider than a regular gauge swatch, but it will save you time in the long run.

Back (make 2)
Ch 42 (45, 48)

ROW 1   Work 2 dc in third ch from hook, *sk next 2 chs, work 3 dc in next ch*. Repeat from * to * across to last 3 chs. Sk next 2 chs, work 1 dc in last ch.

CHICK FEED
No, we didn't say "Holy Cow." We said "Holey Cowl," as in, Check out the cool detachable cowl neck on this simple pullover. This sweater was designed to help with our own winter hot/cold dilemma. Get out of the shower, it's cold . . . bundle up in the sweater, head out shopping . . . it's even colder, add the cowl. Work up a sweat shopping in the mall, remove the cowl. Voila!

ADVANCED BEGINNER

ROW 2   Ch 2 and turn. Work 3 dc in sp between t-ch and first 3-dc cluster. *Work 3 dc between next 2 3-dc clusters*. Repeat from * to * across. Work 1 dc in t-ch.

Repeat Row 2 until panel measures 19 (20, 21, 22)" from the beg. Fasten off.

Sleeves (make 2)
Ch 30 (30, 33, 33)

ROW 1   Work 2 dc in third ch from hook, *sk next 2 chs, work 3 dc in next ch*. Repeat from * to * across to last 3 chs. Sk next 2 chs, work 1 dc in last ch.

ROW 2   Ch 2 and turn. Work 3 dc in sp between t-ch and first 3-dc cluster. *Work 3 dc between next 2 3-dc clusters*. Repeat from * to * across. Work 1 dc in t-ch.

Repeat Row 2 until panel measures 17 (17, 18, 18)" from the beg. Fasten off.

Finishing
Note before finishing: Refer to Lesson 19, "Get It Together," (page 148) for instructions on various finishing techniques.

Using slip stitch seam, beg at sleeve edge, sew front to back along first 5 (5½, 6, 6)" of shoulder seams.

Using mattress stitch, sew sleeve top to armhole, easing to fit. Then sew side and sleeve seams. Weave in all ends.

DETACHABLE COWL

Using larger hook, ch 44

Join with sl st to beginning ch, being careful not to twist chain.

ROUND 1 Ch 3, work 2 dc in same ch as sl st, sk next 2 chs. *Work 3 dc in next ch, sk next 2 chs*. Repeat from * to * around. Join with sl st to beg ch-3.

ROUND 2 Ch 3 and turn. Work 2 dc in sp between t-ch and first 3-dc cluster. *Work 3 dc between next two 3-dc clusters*. Repeat from * to * around. Join with sl st to beg ch-3.

Repeat Round 2 another 7 times. You should have 9 rows total. Fasten off and weave in all yarn ends.

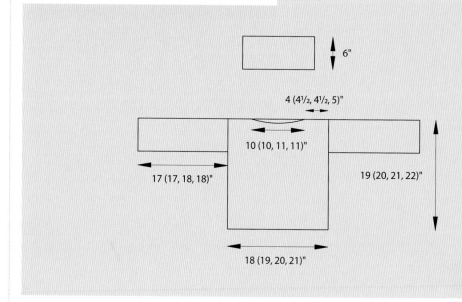

6"

4 (4½, 4½, 5)"

10 (10, 11, 11)"

17 (17, 18, 18)"

19 (20, 21, 22)"

18 (19, 20, 21)"

Okay, true story: Nancy's favorite food (and we mean like the stranded-on-an-island-with-no-other-food favorite) is popcorn. She even knows the different types of kernels like a wine enthusiast knows wine. So one day, while searching for a new popcorn popper online, Nancy took an "Are You a Popologist?" quiz on a popcorn Web site. After she passed the quiz, the site generated a Licensed Popologist diploma, which she printed and framed. It now hangs proudly in her office. This chapter will familiarize you with one of her favorite stitches, the popcorn stitch, a favorite because, well, it resembles popcorn!

Popcorn Stitch

Popcorn stitches add a lot of texture and whimsy to a design. They may be used sparingly in a pattern, as a bauble, or more extensively, as we did in the next project. A Popcorn Stitch is made by working several stitches into the same hole, leaving the last part of the stitch on the hook and then closing them together at the end. Here's how a Popcorn Stitch may be written in a pattern: "Yo, insert hook in next st, yo and pull up a lp, yo and draw through first two lps on hook. *Yo, insert hook into same st, yo and pull up a lp, yo and draw through first two lps on hook*. Repeat from * to * until you have 6 lps on hook. Yo and draw through all 6 lps on hook." Popcorn Stitch completed! When making a Popcorn Stitch you will always be working on the wrong side of your piece; the "popcorn" will pop through on the right side.

pet sheep: there's one in every crowd

completed measurements
3½" x 5"

materials
80 yds/73 m chunky weight mohair in cream (A)

15 yds/14 m DK weight cotton or cotton blend yarn in black (B)

Size I/9 (5.5 mm) crochet hook

Finishing needle

SAMPLE WAS CROCHETED USING PLASSARD "FLORE" (1.75 OZ/ 50 G, 98 YD/90 M PER BALL; 75% KID MOHAIR, 20% WOOL, 5% NYLON) IN CREAM (A) AND PLYMOUTH "WILDFLOWER DK" (1.75 OZ/50 G, 137 YD/125 M PER BALL; 51% COTTON, 49% ACRYLIC) IN BLACK (B).

abbreviation key

beg	beginning
ch	chain
lp	loop
sc	single crochet
st	stitch
yo	yarn over

gauge not necessary

Popcorn Stitch

Yo, insert hook into next st, yo, draw lp through, yo, draw through first 2 lps on hook. *Insert hook into same stitch, yo, draw lp through, yo, draw through 2 lps*. Repeat from * to * until you have 6 lps on hook, yo, draw through 6 lps.

Body

Using yarn A, ch 16

ROW 1   Work 1 sc in second ch from hook and in each ch across, ch 1, turn–15 sc.

ROW 2   *Work 1 popcorn in next sc, 1 sc in next 2 sc*. Repeat from * to* across, ch 1, turn.

ROW 3   1 sc in each sc across, ch 1, turn.

ROW 4   *1 sc in next 2 sc, 1 popcorn in next sc*.

CHICK FEED
Years ago Nancy received an adorable knitted sheep ornament for Christmas. She was so taken with it that she keeps it hanging at home in a prominent spot all year long. Hopefully you will get the same enjoyment from our little lamb. Present it as a cuddly toy for a little one in your life, or add a ribbon and use it as an ornament.

BEGINNER

Repeat from * to * across, ch 1, turn.

ROW 5 1 sc in each sc across, ch 1, turn.

Repeat Rows 2-5 another 5 times. Fasten off.

Fold in half and sew beg and ending rows together to form the body. Fasten off. Thread another yarn through a finishing needle. Weave in and out through one end and cinch the end. Fasten off and repeat for other end.

Head

Using yarn B, ch 2

ROUND 1 Work 5 sc in second ch from hook.

ROUND 2 Work 2 sc in each sc around—10 sc.

ROUND 3 Work 1 sc in next sc, 2 sc in next sc—15 sc.

Fasten off and sew head to one end.

Legs (make 4)

Using yarn B, ch 6

ROW 1 Work 1 sc in second ch from hook and in each ch across—5 sc.

Fasten off and sew legs onto body using horizontal mattress stitch.

Shell Stitch (a.k.a. Fan Stitch)

The shell stitch is a wonderful little technique in the world of crochet-it can turn ordinary yarn into something spectacular. Just as we learned about cluster and popcorn stitches being worked into the same stitch, the shell stitch is worked the same way. What makes it different from the other stitches is that it "fans" across the previous row. There are many patterns available that use shell stitches; they may be used in an allover pattern or to give a beautiful scalloped edge on a garment. Shell stitches have evolved into a wide variety of interesting stitch combinations, ranging from dense, thick stitches to open, lacy ones. If you love making shell stitches, it is wise to invest in a good stitch pattern book.

The stitch pattern below is an example of how to crochet a Shell Stitch. We've used two other variations in this lesson, which are explained in depth in the following projects. Grab some sample yarn and give the Shell Stitch a try: Work 1 sc in next ch, sk next ch, work 5 dc in next ch, sk next 2 chs, work 1 sc in next ch.

surfer chick quick cap

size
One size fits most

completed measurements
Approximately 20" around

materials
104 yd/95 m worsted weight wool or wool blend yarn in varigated color
Size G/7 (4.5 mm) crochet hook

Finishing needle

SAMPLE WAS CROCHETED USING 1 HANK ARTYARNS "SUPERMERINO" (1.75 OZ/50 G, 104 YD/ 95 M PER HANK; 100% HAND-PAINTED MERINO WOOL) IN COLOR 111.

abbreviation key
beg	beginning
ch	chain
dc	double crochet
sc	single crochet
sl st	slip stitch
sp	space

gauge
20 sts to 4" over dc on size 7 (4.5 mm) hook or size needed to obtain gauge

Cap

Ch 4, join with sl st to first ch to form a ring

ROUND 1   Ch 2, work 2 dc in ring, (ch 3, work 3 dc back in same ring) 3 times. Ch 3, join with sl st in top of beg ch-2.

ROUND 2   Ch 2, *work (3 dc, ch 3, 3 dc, ch 3, 1 dc) in next ch-3 sp*. Repeat from * to * another 3 times. Join with sl st to top of beg ch-2.

ROUND 3   Ch 2, *work (3 dc, ch 3, 3 dc, ch 3, 1 dc) in next ch-3 sp*. Repeat from * to * another 7 times. Join with sl st to top of beg ch-2.

ROUND 4   Ch 2, *work (3 dc, ch 2, 1 dc) in next ch-3 sp*. Repeat from * to * around. Join with sl st to top of beg ch-2. 16 clusters made.

ROUND 5   Ch 2, *work (3 dc, ch 2, 1 dc) in next ch-2 sp*. Repeat from * to * around. Join with sl st to top of beg ch-2. 16 clusters made.

Repeat Round 5 another 9 times or to desired length.

LAST ROUND   *Work 1 sc in each of next 3 dc, 2 sc in each ch-2 sp, 1 sc in next dc*. Repeat from * to * around—you should have 96 sts. Fasten off and weave in all yarn ends.

CHICK FEED
This pattern was designed by Nancy's sister, Heather Walpole. This California Chick lives only minutes from a very popular surfing beach, and she noticed that after the surfer girls come off the waves they bundle up in these cute little caps. Ours was made out of alpaca for extra warmth and stretch.

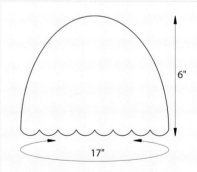

ADVANCED BEGINNER

sensational angora wrap

size
One size fits most

completed measurements
14" x 46"

materials
525 yd/480 m worsted weight angora/wool blend yarn in cream

Size K/10.5 (6.5 mm) crochet hook

Finishing needle

SAMPLE WAS CROCHETED USING NATURALLY "SENSATION" (1.75 OZ/50 G, 131 YD/120 M PER HANK; 70% MERINO, 30% ANGORA) IN CREAM.

abbreviation key

beg	beginning
ch	chain
dc	double crochet
sc	single crochet
sk	skip
sp	space
t-ch	turning chain

gauge
12 sts to 4" over dc on K/10.5 (6.5 mm) hook or size needed to obtain gauge

Wrap

Ch 53

ROW 1 Work 3 dc in fifth ch from hook, sk next 3 chs. *Work 1 sc in next ch, ch 3, work 3 dc in same ch as last sc, skip next 3 chs*. Repeat from * to * across to last ch. Work 1 sc in last ch.

ROW 2 Ch 4 and turn. Work 3 dc in fourth ch from hook. *Work 1 sc in next ch-3 sp, ch 3, work 3 dc in same ch-3 sp as last sc*. Repeat from * to * across. Work 1 sc in ch-4 t-ch.

Repeat Row 2 until panel measures 46" from the beg.

Fasten off and weave in all yarn ends. Attach button approximately 8" up from finished edge and 2 ½" in from side. Since lace openings are large, it is not necessary to make a buttonhole.

Button placement

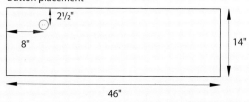

ADVANCED BEGINNER

CHICK FEED
This adorable and functional wrap is perfect for throwing over just about anything. Think of it as a stylish little blankie for your shoulders. It's great to have at the office when the AC is blasting, for evening when there's a chill in the air, or just to add a little polish to an outfit.

Front Post and Back Post Double Crochet

One of the wonderful things about crochet is its versatility. So far we've been crocheting stitches by working into the stitch made on the previous row. But we don't have to crochet only in one spot. What if we tried making stitches in the front or back of a stitch? We would end up with stitches that look like basket weave, cables, or even ribbing. The main difference is that you won't be working through any loops. Instead, you'll work the stitch in the row below, which is called working around the post of a stitch. It works best with double crochet or triple crochet stitches.

Front Post Double Crochet (FPdc)

These stitches are a variation of double crochet. They are worked exactly the same way, with one exception. Instead of inserting the hook under the heart to make a stitch, insert the hook around the post immediately below the heart you would normally work into.

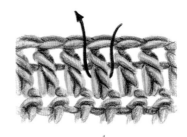

1

Let's practice making a front post double crochet. To begin, make a foundation chain and a row of double crochet. On the next row you will work a FPdc around each of the stitches as follows: Yarn over, insert the hook from front to back on the right side of the post (1), yarn over and pull up a loop, yarn over and draw through first two loops on hook, yarn over and draw through last two loops on hook (2).

Back Post Double Crochet (BPdc)

A back post double crochet only varies from the front post double crochet in that you work the stitch on the wrong side of your work instead of on the right side. Let's practice making a back post double crochet. To begin, make a foundation chain and a row of double crochet. On the next row you will work a BPdc around each of the stitches as follows: Yarn over, insert the hook from front to back on the wrong side of the post (3), yarn over and pull up a loop, yarn over and draw through first two loops on hook, yarn over and draw through last two loops on hook (4).

Now that you have learned to make both front post and back post double crochets, try your skills on the Boyfriend Basket Weave Scarf. This scarf is made like a checkerboard: You will work across the row by alternating between FPdc and BPdc, then reversing the combination.

2

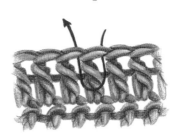

3

4

| the boyfriend basket weave scarf |

size
One size fits most

completed measurements
Approximately 5½" x 56"

materials
330 yd/301 m light chunky weight alpaca, wool, or wool blend yarn in charcoal

Size K/10.5 (6.5 mm crochet hook)

Finishing needle

SAMPLE WAS CROCHETED USING PLYMOUTH "BABY ALPACA BRUSH" (50 G/1.7 OZ, 110 YD/100 M PER BALL; 80% BABY ALPACA, 20% ACRYLIC) IN CHARCOAL #402.

abbreviation key

beg	beginning
BPdc	back post double crochet
ch	chain
dc	double crochet
hdc	half double crochet
FPdc	front post double crochet
sk	skip
st(s)	stitch(es)

gauge
14 sts to 4" over dc on size K/10.5 (6.5 mm) hook or size needed to obtain gauge

Scarf
Ch 22

ROW 1   Work 1 dc in fourth ch from hook and in each ch across, ch 2 (counts as first st on next row, now and throughout), turn—20 dc.

ROW 2   Sk first dc, *work 1 FPdc around each of next 3 dc, work 1 BPdc around each of next 3 dc*. Repeat from * to * across. 1 hdc in top of beg ch. Ch 2, turn.

ROW 3   Sk first hdc, *work 1 FPdc around next 3 sts, 1 BPdc around next 3 sts*. Repeat from * to * across. 1 hdc in top of beg ch. Ch 2, turn.

ROW 4   Sk first hdc, *work 1 BPdc around next 3 sts, work 1 FPdc around next 3 sts. Repeat from * to * across. 1 hdc in top of beg ch. Ch 2, turn.

ROW 5   Repeat Row 4.

ROW 6   Repeat Row 3.

Repeat Rows 3-6 until panel measures 56" from the beg. Fasten off and weave in all yarn ends.

ADVANCED BEGINNER

CHICK FEED

If you've gotten this far into the book, you probably have someone special in your life who has been watching you fiendishly crochet some pretty cool projects—and eventually that person will ask when you will make something for him or her! The Boyfriend Basket Weave Scarf is a fabulous project for just about everyone. This richly textured pattern will keep your interest piqued throughout, and you'll be amazed at the great results and the compliments. Ours was made out of a brushed alpaca for extra warmth and softness.

Backstitching

Backstitching may be used to stitch a very sturdy seam or as an embellishment. It is often used for seaming an item that requires very little stretch. For this reason it works well for many felted projects. We tend to avoid this stitch for finishing garments because it can be rather bulky and there are other finishing choices that are more suitable. See Lesson 19 on finishing techniques.

To backstitch, thread your needle with a strand of yarn and attach it to the starting point by making 2 or 3 stitches in the same place. Do you know the old saying "Two steps forward, one step back"? That is what you will be doing to make this stitch! Insert the needle 2 stitches past the starting point and draw through. Now go into the stitch one step back from where you just came up and come up 1 step forward of that stitch. Keep repeating this step until you have worked across the stitches. Fasten off and weave in all yarn ends.

bad to the bone dog jacket

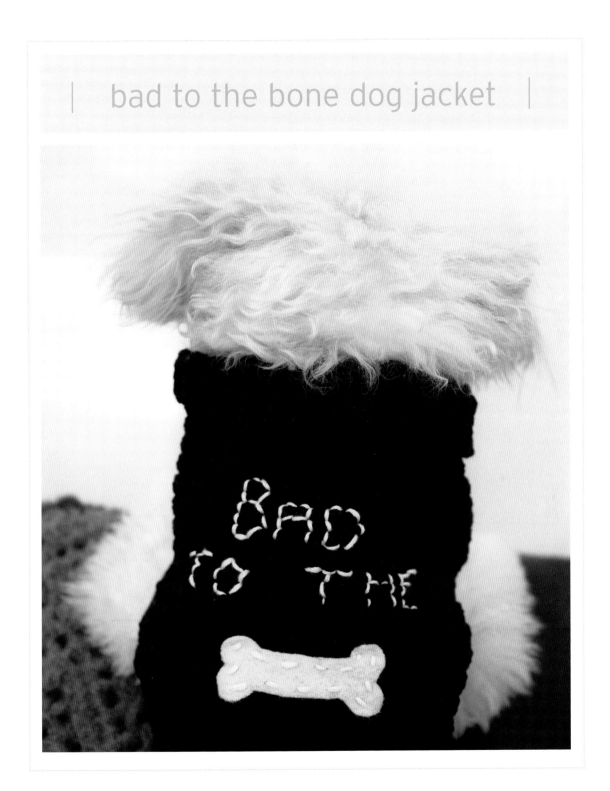

sizes

Small (Medium, Large)

Yorkie type (Shih Tzu type,
Jack Russell type)

completed chest measurements

$14\frac{1}{2}$ ($16\frac{1}{4}$, $18\frac{1}{2}$)"

completed length measurements

6 ($6\frac{1}{2}$, 7)"

materials

100 (120, 140) yd/91 (109, 128) m
worsted weight yarn, preferably
washable in black (A)

3 yd/2.7 m scrap yarn or
embroidery floss in cream (B)

One 9" x 12" soft felt
rectangle in cream

Size I/9 (5.5 mm) crochet hook

Finishing needle

SAMPLE WAS CROCHETED USING SKEIN
KEY WEST KARIBBEAN KOTTON (1.75
OZ/50 G, 74 YD/68 M PER BALL; 100%
MERCERIZED COTTON) IN BLACK.

abbreviation key

ch	chain
sc	single crochet
sc2tog	single crochet two stitches together
sk	skip
st(s)	stitch(es)

gauge

15 sts and 20 rows to 4" over
sc on size I/9 (5.5 mm) hook
or size needed to obtain gauge

Coat

RIBBED COLLAR

Ch 5 (5, 6)

ROW 1 Work 1 sc in second ch from hook and in each ch across—4 (4, 5) sc.

ROW 2 Ch 1 and turn. Work 1 sc in each sc across in BACK LOOPS only.

Repeat Row 2 another 38 (43, 50) times. You should have 40 (45, 52) rows total. Finish off.

BODY

Attach yarn to side edge and work 1 sc in each of 40 (45, 52) rows—40 (45, 52) sc.

ROW 1 Ch 1 and turn. Work 1 sc in each sc across.

ROW 2 Ch 1 and turn. Work 2 sc in first st, 1 sc in each st across to last st, 2 sc in last st—42 (47, 54) sc.

Repeat Rows 1 and 2 another 6 (7, 8) times ending with 54 (61, 70) sts.

Armhole Openings

ROW 1 Ch 1 and turn. Work 1 sc in each sc across.

ROW 2 Ch 1 and turn. Work 1 sc in each of next 5 (6, 7) sc. Set this ball of yarn down. Sk next 9 (10, 11) sts. Attach a new ball of yarn and work 1 sc in each of next 26 (29, 34) sc. Set this ball of yarn down. Sk next 9 (10, 11) sts. Attach a new ball of yarn and work 1 sc in each of last 5 (6, 7) sc.

ROW 3 Ch 1 and turn. Work 1 sc in 5 (6, 7) sc. Set this ball down. Pick up next ball. Ch 1 and work 1 sc in next 26 (29, 34) sc. Set this ball down. Pick up next ball. Ch 1 and work 1 sc in last 5 (6, 7) sc.

Repeat Row 3 another 6 (7, 9) times— 9 (10, 12) rows completed.

ROW 13 Ch 1 and turn. Work 1 sc in each of next 5 (6, 7) sc, ch 9 (10, 11) and work 1 sc in each of next 26 (29, 34) sc, ch 9 (10, 11) and work 1 sc in each of next 5 (6, 7) sc.

ROW 14 Ch 1 and turn. Work 1 sc in each sc and ch across—54 (61, 70) sc.

ROW 15 Ch 1 and turn. Work 1 sc in each sc across—54 (61, 70) sc.

Repeat Row 15 another 6 (8, 10) times. To make jacket longer or shorter to fit your dog, work more or fewer rows here, depending on your dog's size.

Fasten off and weave in all yarn ends.

Join side seams using vertical mattress stitch. Do not sew collar closed.

Jacket "Sleeves"

Attach yarn at leg opening and work 7 (9, 11) sc around each edge of leg opening – 28 (36, 44) sts.

SIZE SMALL: Begin on Row 5.
SIZE MEDIUM: Begin on Row 3.
SIZE LARGE: Begin on Row 1.

ROW 1 *Work 1 sc in next 9 sc, sc2tog over next 2 sts*. Repeat from * to * around—40 sts.

ROW 2 *Work 1 sc in next 8 sc, sc2tog over next 2 sts*. Repeat from * to * around—36 sts.

ROW 3 *Work 1 sc in next 7 sc, sc2tog over next 2 sts*. Repeat from * to * around—32 sts.

ROW 4 *Work 1 sc in next 6 sc, sc2tog over next 2 sts*. Repeat from * to * around—28 sts.

ROW 5 *Work 1 sc in next 5 sc, sc2tog over next 2 sts*. Repeat from * to * around—24 sts.

ROW 6 *Work 1 sc in next 4 sc, sc2tog over next 2 sts*. Repeat from * to * around—20 sts.

ROW 7 Work 1 sc in each sc around.

ROW 8 Work 1 sc in each sc around.

Fasten off and repeat on other leg opening.

Back Design

Using yarn B, backstitch letters as noted on chart below.

Trace and cut out dog bone. Stitch to jacket back.

Fasten off and weave in all yarn ends.

diva dog tutu

**Small (Medium, Large)
Yorkie type (Shih Tzu type,
Jack Russell type)**

14 (17, 24)"

11 (16, 18)"

**300 (350, 375) yd/
274 (320, 343) m DK
weight cotton or cotton
blend yarn in light pink (A)**

**90 yd/82 m DK weight
cotton or cotton blend yarn
in bright pink (B)**

**Size I/9 (5.5 mm) crochet
hook**

Finishing needle

SAMPLE WAS CROCHETED USING
PLYMOUTH WILDFLOWER DK
(1.75 OZ/50 G, 137 YD/126 M PER
BALL; 51% COTTON, 49% ACRYLIC)
IN BUBBLEGUM AND BRIGHT PINK.

beg	beginning
ch	chain
dc	double crochet
sc	single crochet
Sc2tog	single crochet two together
st(s)	stitch(es)

**16 sts and 20 rows to 4"
over sc using size I/9
(5.5 mm) hook or size
needed to obtain gauge**

Tutu

NECK EDGE

Using yarn A, ch 47 (56, 66)

ROW 1   Work 1 sc in second ch from hook and in each ch across–46 (55, 65) sts.

ROW 2   Ch 1 and turn. Work 1 sc in each sc across.

ROW 3   Ch 1 and turn. Work 1 sc in each sc across.

Continue working in sc and shape chest as follows: Increase 1 st at each end of next and following 2nd (4th, 1st) row 4 (6, 15) times more to 56 (69, 97) sts. Work evenly in sc until panel measures 3 (6, 5½)" from the beg.

Continue working in sc and shape back as follows: Skip last 11 (13, 19) sts at the END of the next 2 rows. Work 2 more rows of sc. Decrease 1 st at each end of next and every other row 4 (6, 9) times until 24 (29, 39) sts remain. Work even until panel measures 10 (15, 17)" from the beg. Fasten off and weave in all yarn ends.

Finishing

Fold in half lengthwise and sew seam from neck to top of legs using vertical mattress stitch.

Using yarn B, work 1 round sc around neckline edge. Now work 1 round sc around neckline edge. Fasten off and weave in all yarn ends.

Using yarn B, work 3 rows dc around leg and back opening.

Fasten off and weave in all yarn ends.

CHICK FEED

Dress your darling like the diva that she is! We crocheted this little sweater in a washable cotton/acrylic blend. Small dogs come in all shapes and sizes. You may need to add or subtract stitches or rows to custom fit your pooch.

125

ADVANCED BEGINNER

Overstitching

This is a quick, easy way to add color and pizzazz to a single crochet sweater or bag. Here's how it's done: Make a swatch of single crochet fabric. Thread a needle with a 24-inch length of yarn in a contrasting color. Starting from the back of the fabric, bring the needle up from the lower left corner of a stitch. Then insert the needle down into the upper right corner of the same stitch (1). Bring the needle up from the lower right corner of the stitch and insert the needle down into the upper left corner of the same stitch. Continue making X's by repeating the steps (2). Fasten off and weave in all yarn ends in the back of your work.

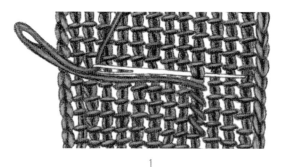

1

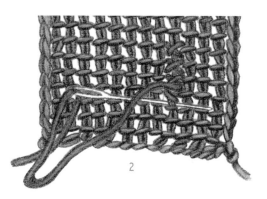

2

Single Crochet Edge

Sometimes you'll want the edge of a project to look a little more polished or to have a contrasting color. A single crochet edge does the trick. It's also a good technique to use if an edge is too loose. You'll find that just a row or two of single crochet will stabilize a neckline or edge quite nicely. Here's how it's done: Make a slip knot and attach the yarn to the edge of the garment using a slip stitch. Work 1 single crochet in the edge of each stitch or hole evenly across the garment. Fasten off and weave in all yarn ends.

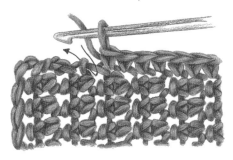

Picot Edge

Picot edge gives a cute little ruffle without being too frilly. It is worked around the edge after a garment is completed. Attach the yarn to the garment edge with a single crochet, evenly working the picot edge as follows: *chain 3, 1 sc in next sp*. Repeat from * to * around the garment edges. Fasten off and weave in all yarn ends.

chicks' felted zebra slippers

sizes
Women's average sizes 7-9

completed measurements
Approximately 7½" x 14" before felting

Approximately 5" x 9½" after felting

materials
260 yd/238 m medium weight wool suitable for felting in black (A)

130 yd/118 m medium weight wool suitable for felting in cream (B)

130 yd/118 m medium weight wool suitable for felting in green (C)

Size N/15 (10.0 mm) crochet hook

2 plastic grocery bags (for shaping)

1 sheet craft foam, 1½" thick and approximately 10" x 12"

Finishing needle

SAMPLE WAS CROCHETED USING MANOS DEL URUGUAY "WOOL" (3.5 OZ/100 G, 138 YD/126 M PER BALL; 100% PURE WOOL) IN BLACK, CREAM, AND CITRIC.

abbreviation key
beg	beginning
ch	chain
inc	increase
sc	single crochet
sc2tog	single crochet two together

gauge
8 sts to 4" over sc on size N/15 (10.0 mm) hook or size needed to obtain gauge

CHICK FEED
These fun felted slippers are a quick project and make a great gift! We crocheted them using our favorite color combination, zebra stripes and lime green. Don't let the zebra stripes intimidate you: it's not as if we had little balls of black and cream yarn everywhere to make these. First we crocheted the top strap in cream and then simply overstitched the zebra pattern in black right on top of it.

BEGINNER

Bag

TOP STRAP (MAKE 2)

Using yarn B, ch 18

ROW 1 Work 1 sc in second ch from hook and in each ch across—17 sc.

ROW 2 Ch 1 and turn. Work 1 sc in each sc across.

Repeat Row 2 another 13 times. You should have 15 rows total. Fasten off.

Following the photograph, overstitch zebra pattern onto Top Straps using yarn A.

BOTTOM (MAKE 4)

Using yarn A, ch 10

ROW 1 Work 1 sc in second ch from hook and in each ch across—9 sc.

ROW 2 Ch 1 and turn. Inc 1 sc at the beg and end of row—11 sc.

ROW 3 Ch 1 and turn. Work 1 sc in each sc across—11 sc.

ROW 4 Ch 1 and turn. Inc 1 sc at the beg and end of row—13 sc.

ROWS 5-8 Ch 1 and turn. Work 1 sc in each sc across—13 sc.

ROW 9 Ch 1 and turn. Inc 1 sc at the beg and end of row—15 sc.

ROWS 10-17 Ch 1 and turn. Work 1 sc in each sc across—15 sc.

ROW 18 Ch 1 and turn. Sc2tog at the beg and end of row—13 sc.

ROWS 19-24 Ch 1 and turn. Work 1 sc in each sc across—13 sc.

ROW 25 Ch 1 and turn. Sc2tog at the beg and end of row—11 sc.

ROWS 26-30 Ch 1 and turn. Work 1 sc in each sc across—11 sc.

ROW 31 Ch 1 and turn. Sc2tog at the beg and end of row—9 sc.

ROWS 32-35 Ch 1 and turn. Work 1 sc in each sc across—9 sc.

Fasten off.

2 Lower and 2 Upper Soles made.

Slipper Construction

1. Using Lower Sole and yarn A, work 33 sc evenly along one long side, 7 sc evenly along short side, 33 sc evenly along other long side, 7 sc evenly along last short side—80 sc. Place marker to mark the beg of round.

2. Continuing in sc work 2 more rounds. Lower Sole will now be larger than Upper Sole to allow for stuffing later.

3. NEXT ROUND Attach Upper Sole to Lower Sole by working 1 more round of sc. Leave heel open to add foam after felting. Fasten off.

4. Using yarn C, work 1 round in sc. Fasten off. Repeat for second slipper. Weave in all yarn ends.

5. Using yarn C, work 1 round in sc around outside edges of Top Strap. Repeat for second Top Strap. Weave in all yarn ends.

6. Attach Top Strap. Edge of strap

should be approximately 4 rows down from toe end of soles. Whipstitch sides in place (see page 149). Weave in all yarn ends.

Finishing

Felt slippers as shown in Lesson 10 (page 75). Once slippers have been felted and while they're still wet, shape slippers by filling space between Upper and Lower Sole with plastic bags. Let dry. Cut foam to shape of sole (make 2), slip in foam, and sew closed using whipstitch.

11 (14)" before felting
10 (12)" after felting

7 (7)" before felting
4 (5½)" after felting

game day tee

sizes
Small (Medium, Large, X-Large)

Fits bust sizes
32 (34, 36, 38)"

completed chest measurements
31 (33, 35, 37)"

materials
375 (375, 500, 500) yd/343 (343, 457, 457) m heavy worsted weight angora, wool, or wool blend yarn in chocolate brown (A)

120 (120, 240, 240) yd/110 (110, 219, 219) m heavy worsted weight angora, wool, or wool blend yarn in periwinkle (B)

Size I/9 (5.5 mm) crochet hook

SAMPLE WAS CROCHETED USING CLASSIC ELITE "LUSH" (1.75 OZ/ 50 G, 124 YD/113 M PER HANK; 50% ANGORA, 50% WOOL) IN CHOCOLATE BROWN (A) AND PERIWINKLE (B).

abbreviation key
beg	beginning
ch	chain
dc	double crochet
dc2tog	double crochet two together
sc	single crochet
sk	skip
st(s)	stitch(es)

gauge
14 sts and 9 rows to 4" over dc using size I/9 (5.5 mm) hook or size needed to obtain gauge

Back

Using yarn A, ch 58 (62, 65, 69)

ROW 1   Work 1 dc in third ch from hook and in each ch across—56 (60, 63, 67) dc.

ROW 2   Ch 2 and turn. Work 1 dc in each dc across.

Repeat Row 2 another 26 (28, 28, 28) times. You should have 28 (30, 30, 30) rows total.

Work armhole shaping as follows:
NEXT 2 ROWS   Ch 2 and turn. Work 1 dc in each dc across to last 3 sts. Skip last 3 sts.

CHICK FEED
We made this cool base-ball T-shirt using all double crochet. The two colors give it a relaxed, weekend style. For a little more polish, try crocheting it all in one color.

ADVANCED BEGINNER

Note decreases as follows: Dc2tog at armhole ends of every other row 7 (6, 5, 5) times, then dc2tog at armhole ends of every row 2 (4, 6, 8) times. Continue working in dc for 16 (16, 16, 18) rows total from beg of armhole shaping. You should have 36 (38, 39, 39) sts remaining.

Continuing in dc, work neck shaping for each size noted below.

Work both sides at the same time. Work 1 dc in each of next 6 dc. Sk next 24 (26, 27, 27) sts. Attach another ball of yarn and work 1 dc in each of next 6 dc.

Dc2tog at neck edge of every row twice until 2 sts remain. Fasten off.

Front

Using yarn A, ch 58 (62, 65, 69)

ROW 1 Work 1 dc in third ch from hook and in each ch across–56 (60, 63, 67) dc.

ROW 2 Ch 2 and turn. Work 1 dc in each dc across.

Repeat Row 2 another 26 (28, 28, 28) times. You should have 28 (30, 30, 30) rows total.

Work armhole shaping as follows:
NEXT 2 ROWS   Ch 2 and turn. Work 1 dc in each dc across to last 3 sts. Skip last 3 sts.

Note decreases as follows: Dc2tog at armhole ends of every other row 7 (6, 5, 5) times, then dc2tog at armhole ends

of every row 2 (4, 6, 8) times. Continue until you have worked 10 (10, 10, 12) rows total from beg of armhole shaping. You should have 42 (46, 49, 51) sts remaining.
Shape neckline as follows, continuing raglan shaping AT THE SAME TIME:

Continuing in dc, work neck shaping for each size noted below.

Work both sides at the same time. Work 1 dc in each of next 12 (14, 15, 16) dc. Sk next 18 (18, 19, 19) sts. Attach another ball of yarn and work 1 dc in each of next 12 (14, 15, 16) dc.

Dc2tog at neck edge of every row 6 times, until 2 sts remain. Fasten off.

SLEEVES (MAKE 2)

Using yarn B, ch 37 (38, 39, 41)

ROW 1 Work 1 dc in third ch from hook and in each ch across–35 (36, 37, 39) dc.

ROW 2 Ch 2 and turn. Work 1 dc in each dc across.

Continue working in dc, shaping as follows:

Inc 1 sc at each end of every 6th (4th, 4th, 4th) row 1 (2, 2, 2) times to 37 (40, 41, 43) sts. You should have 6 (8, 8, 8) rows total.

Work evenly in dc for 6 (4, 4, 4) more rows. You should have 12 rows total.

Continuing in dc, begin raglan shaping as follows: Skip last 3 sts at the end of the next 2 rows.

Size Small: Dc2tog at each end of every 2nd row twice, then dc2tog at each end of every row 12 times. You should have 3 sts remaining. Fasten off.

Sizes Medium and Large: Dc2tog at each end of every row 16 times. You should have 2 sts remaining. Fasten off.

Size X-Large: Dc2tog at each end of every 2nd row once, then dc2tog at each end of every row 16 times. You should have 3 sts remaining. Fasten off.

Finishing

Note before finishing: Refer to Lesson 19, "Get It Together," (page 148) for instructions on various finishing techniques.

Using mattress stitch, sew sleeves to front and back along raglan armhole seams. Then sew sleeve top to armhole, easing to fit. Next sew side and sleeve seams. Weave in all yarn ends.

Using yarn B, work 2 rows sc evenly around neckline edge.

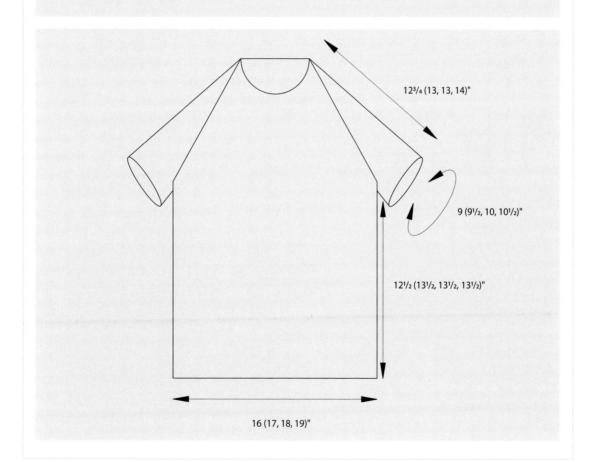

12³/₄ (13, 13, 14)"

9 (9¹/₂, 10, 10¹/₂)"

12¹/₂ (13¹/₂, 13¹/₂, 13¹/₂)"

16 (17, 18, 19)"

posh ballet wrap

sizes

Small (Medium, Large, X-Large)

Fits bust size
32 (36, 38, 40)"

completed chest measurements

36 (40, 44, 46)"

materials

875 (1,000, 1,125, 1,250) yd/800 (914, 1,028, 1,143) m worsted weight wool or wool blend yarn in pink

Size I/9 (5.5 mm) crochet hook

Finishing needle

SAMPLE WAS CROCHETED USING CLASSIC ELITE "POSH" (1.75 OZ/50 G, 125 YD/114 M PER HANK; 30% CASHMERE, 70% SILK) IN BALLET PINK.

abbreviation key

ch	chain
dc	double crochet
dc2tog	double crochet two together
sc	single crochet
sk	skip
sp	space
st(s)	stitch(es)

gauge

12 sts and 8 rows to 4" over dc using size I/9 (5.5 mm) hook or size needed to obtain gauge

Back

Ch 56 (62, 66, 70)

ROW 1   Work 1 dc in third ch from hook and in each ch across–54 (60, 64, 68) sts.

ROW 2   Ch 2 and turn. Work 1 dc in each dc across.

Repeat Row 2 for another 21 rows. Panel should measure approximately 12" from the beginning.

Continuing in dc work armhole shaping for each size noted below as follows: Sk the last 2 (3, 3, 4) sts and the end of the next 2 rows.

Size Small: Dc2tog at each end of Rows 26, 27, 28, 32, and 40.

Size Medium: Dc2tog at each end of Rows 26, 27, 29, 30, 33, 39, and 40.

CHICK FEED

Be a ballerina . . . or just look like one! Our ballet wrap with 3/4-length sleeves works up very quickly in double crochet. We've trimmed it with an adorable picot edge and added a side tie. You may want to substitute silk ribbon for the ties for extra embellishment. We crocheted our wrap with a silk/cashmere blend yarn so it feels as soft as it looks.

ADVANCED BEGINNER

Size Large: Dc2tog at each end of Rows 26, 27, 29, 30, and 33.

Size X-Large: Dc2tog at each end of Rows 26, 27, 29, and 30.

All sizes: Continue until there are 42 rows from the beg—40 (42, 50, 56) sts remain. Fasten off and weave in all yarn ends.

Front (make 2)

Ch 40 (43, 46, 48)

ROW 1   Work 1 dc in third ch from hook and in each ch across—38 (41, 44, 46) sts.

ROW 2   Ch 2 and turn. Work 1 dc in each dc across.

Continuing in dc work neck and armhole for each size noted below as follows:

Size Small: Dc2tog at neck edge of next row, then every other row 19 times. At the same time, work armhole shaping: Sk the last 2 (3, 3, 4) sts at the end of Row 25.

Continuing in dc work armhole shaping for each size noted below as follows:

Size Small: Dc2tog at armhole edge of Rows 26, 27, 28, 32, and 40.

Size Medium: Dc2tog at armhole edge of Rows 26, 27, 29, 30, 33, 39, and 40.

Size Large: Dc2tog at armhole edge of Rows 26, 27, 29, 30, and 33.

Size X-Large: Dc2tog at armhole edge of Rows 26, 27, 29, and 30.

All sizes: Continue until there are 42 rows from the beg—11 (11, 16, 18) sts remain. Fasten off and weave in all yarn ends.

Sleeves (make 2)

Ch 28 (30, 30, 32)

ROW 1   Work 1 dc in third ch from hook and in each ch across—26 (28, 28, 30) sts.

ROW 2   Ch 2 and turn. Work 1 dc in each dc across.

Continuing in dc, work increases as follows: Increase 1 st at each end of Rows 4, 8, 16, 20, 24, 27, and 31.

Shape Cap as follows:
Sk the last 3 sts at the end of Rows 34 and 35.

Dc2tog 2 times at each end of Rows 36 and 37.

Finishing

Note before finishing: Refer to Lesson 19, "Get It Together," (page 148) for instructions on various finishing techniques.

Using horizontal mattress stitch, sew fronts to back along shoulder seams.

Using mattress stitch, sew sleeves to fronts and back. Then sew side seams.

Weave in all yarn ends.

PICOT EDGE

Attach yarn to bottom front with a sc, evenly work picot edge as follows: *ch 3, 1 sc in next sp*. Repeat from * to * around front and neckline edge. Fasten off and weave in all yarn ends.

Wrap Ties

TIE 1   Ch 30. Beginning in 2nd ch from hook, work 1 sc in each ch across. Fasten off. Using tails, attach Tie to one front point.

TIE 2   Ch 100. Beginning in 2nd ch from hook, work 1 sc in each ch across. Fasten off. Using tail, attach Tie to other front point.

Weave in all yarn ends.

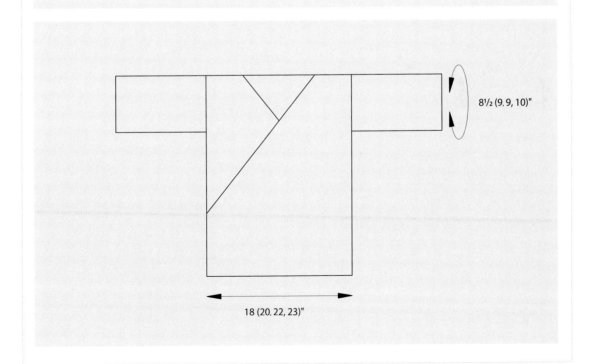

8¹⁄₂ (9, 9, 10)"

18 (20, 22, 23)"

pocket full of posies felted purse

completed measurements

13" x 9" base before felting

9 x 6½" after felting (completed project will shrink by approximately one third its original size)

materials

230 yd/210 m light chunky weight wool for felting in green (A)

100 yd/91 m light chunky weight wool for felting in pink (B)

100 yd/91 m light chunky weight wool for felting in fuchsia (C)

Size K/10.5 (6.5 mm) crochet hook

Size L/11 (8.0 mm) crochet hook

Finishing needle

SAMPLE SHOWN WAS CROCHETED WITH ANOS DEL URUGUAY WOOL (3.5 OZ/100 G, 138 YD/126 M PER HANK; 100% PURE WOOL) IN CITRIC, PINK, AND FUCHSIA.

abbreviation key

beg	beginning
ch	chain
sc	single crochet
sc2tog	single crochet two together

gauge

11 sts and 14 rows to 4" over sc using size L/11 (8.0 mm) hook, or size needed to obtain gauge

Handbag Base

NOTE: MARK BEGINNING OF ROUNDS WITH A SAFETY PIN OR PIECE OF YARN. ROUNDS ARE WORKED CONTINUOUSLY.

Using larger hook and yarn A, ch 2

ROUND 1   Work 6 sc in second ch from hook.

ROUND 2   Work 2 sc in each sc—12 sc.

ROUND 3   *1 sc in next sc, 2 sc in next sc*. Repeat from * to * around—18 sc.

ROUND 4   *1 sc in next sc, 2 sc in next sc*. Repeat from * to * around—27 sc.

CHICK FEED

This little evening bag is just big enough to hold lipstick, powder, and maybe a few unmentionables. The base is crocheted first and then felted. Add the handle and embellish with flowers.

ADVANCED BEGINNER

ROUND 5   *1 sc in next 2 sc, 2 sc in next sc*. Repeat from * to * around—36 sc.

ROUND 6   1 sc in each sc.

ROUND 7   *1 sc in next 3 sc, 2 sc in next sc*. Repeat from * to * around—45 sc.

ROUND 8   1 sc in each sc.

ROUND 9   1 sc in each sc.

ROUND 10   1 sc in each sc.

ROUND 11   *1 sc in next 4 sc, 2 sc in next sc*. Repeat from * to * around—54 sc.

ROUND 12   1 sc in each sc.

ROUND 13   1 sc in each sc.

ROUND 14   1 sc in each sc.

ROUND 15   *1 sc in next 5 sc, 2 sc in next sc*. Repeat from * to * around—63 sc.

ROUND 16   1 sc in each sc.

ROUND 17   1 sc in each sc.

ROUND 18   *1 sc in next 6 sc, 2 sc in next sc*. Repeat from * to * around—72 sc.

ROUND 19   1 sc in each sc.

ROUND 20   1 sc in each sc.

ROUND 21   *1 sc in next 6 sc, sc2tog over next 2 sts*. Repeat from * to * around—63 sc.

ROUND 22   1 sc in each sc.

ROUND 23   1 sc in each sc.

ROUND 24   *1 sc in next 5 sc, sc2tog over next 2 sts*. Repeat from * to * around—54 sc.

ROUND 25   1 sc in each sc.

ROUND 26   *1 sc in next 4 sc, sc2tog over next 2 sts*. Repeat from * to * around—45 sc.

ROUND 27   1 sc in each sc.

ROUND 28   1 sc in each sc.

ROUND 29   *1 sc in next 3 sc, sc2tog over next 2 sts*. Repeat from * to * around—36 sc.

ROUND 30   1 sc in each sc.
Fasten off and weave in yarn ends.

Cord Handle
Using yarn A, ch 4

ROW 1   Work 1 sc in second ch from hook and in each ch across.

ROW 2   Ch 1 and turn. Work 1 sc in each sc across.

Repeat Row 2 until handle measures 12" from the beg.

Fasten off and weave in all yarn ends.

Follow felting instructions in Lesson 10 (page 75).

Flower

Make 15 flowers total:

8 flowers using yarn B, 7 flowers using yarn C

Using smaller hook and yarn A, ch 42

ROW 1 1 dc in 4th ch from hook, *ch 1, 1 dc in next ch*. Repeat from * to * across—40 dc.

ROW 2 Ch 1 and turn. In the first ch-1 sp work (1 sc, ch 1, 5 dc, ch 1, 1 sc), *1 sc in next ch-1 sp, in next ch-1 sp work (1 sc, ch 1, 5 dc, ch 1, 1 sc)*. Repeat from * to * across (20 petals made). Fasten off, leaving an 18" tail.

Finishing

Thread tail through finishing needle to sew flower. Begin at tail end and sew 2 petals together at base to form center of flower. Spiral the remaining coil of petals around bud to form a flower. Sew together by stitching layers at the base. Using yarn, sew onto bag using whipstitch.

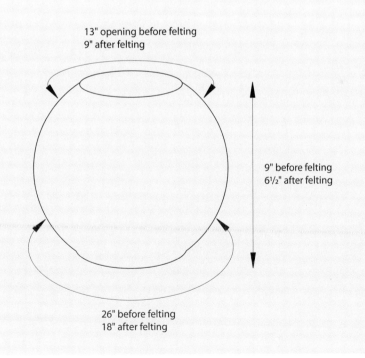

13" opening before felting
9" after felting

9" before felting
6½" after felting

26" before felting
18" after felting

Double the Pleasure, Double the Fun

We've really covered a lot of information up to this point. So, just like you cram for a test in school, we are going to double up on a few new techniques and cram them into one chapter because, quite frankly, we think you're ready for it! This lesson includes an all-in-one piece sweater technique called top-down construction and instructions for how to make buttonholes. You will then be able to try out your new skills with Heather's Café Cardigan.

Top-Down Construction

Do you hate to sew a lot of seams? Then this lesson and accompanying cardigan project are for you! The Café Cardigan is made using the top-down method. A top-down sweater begins at the neckline and forms the front, back, and sleeves all at the same time, until you reach the underarms. Then you work down the body until you reach the desired length of the garment. The final part of the process is to reattach the yarn at the sleeve edges to finish the sleeves. The only seaming involved is for the sleeve seams. One reason the top-down method is so useful is that it allows you to adjust the length for a perfect fit. Another plus is that you can try on the garment periodically as you work and add or decrease rows in the body or sleeves. Follow the pattern carefully and watch your top-down sweater take shape!

Making Buttonholes

Making buttonholes in crochet is not as daunting as one would think. In fact, by this point you already have all the skills you need! The two most common ways to make a buttonhole are the Button Loop method and the Two Row Buttonhole method.

BUTTON LOOP METHOD

A button loop extends from the garment and loops around the button for closure. Button loops are not quite as stable as the Two Row method, but they may be the most appropriate, depending on the style of your garment or project. For example, attaching a button and button loop to one of the bag projects shown in this book will help hold it shut and serve as an attractive embellishment.

Here's how it's done:

1.   Attach button to garment in desired location.
2.   To attach and make the loop, attach yarn to desired starting point using a slip stitch, make a chain long enough to go around the button and back to the starting point. You may need to experiment to figure out how many chains you'll need.
3.   When you've made the correct number of chains to suit your button, attach the other end at the starting point with a slip stitch. Fasten off and weave in all yarn ends.

TWO ROW BUTTONHOLE METHOD

This is the most common way of making buttonholes. Most patterns using this method will usually include instructions, but we want to familiarize you with the technique so you understand the mechanics of a buttonhole.

We'll work this buttonhole in single crochet.

Ch 10

ROW 1   Work 1 sc in second ch from hook and in each ch across.

ROW 2   Ch 1 and turn. Work 1 sc in each of next 3 sc. Sk next 3 sc, ch 3, work 3 sc in each of last 3 sc—buttonhole row.

ROW 3   Ch 1 and turn. Work 1 sc in each of next 3 sc, work 3 sc in ch-3 sp, work 3 sc in each of last 3 sc—buttonhole completed!

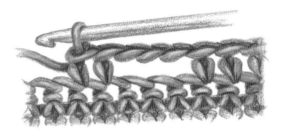

| heather's café cardigan |

size
Small (Medium, Large,
X-Large)

finished chest measurements
32 (36, 40, 43½)"

materials
850 (970, 1,100, 1,250)
yd/ 777(887, 1,006,
1,143) m light chunky
weight wool or wool blend
yarn in pink

Size I/9 (5.50 mm)
crochet hook

7 buttons of your choice

Finishing needle

SAMPLE WAS CROCHETED USING
MANOS DEL URUGUAY WOOL
(3.5 OZ/100 G, 138 YD/126 M PER
HANK; 100% PURE WOOL) IN
BRIGHT PINK.

abbreviation key

beg	beginning
ch(s)	chain (s)
ch-sp	chain-space
dc	double crochet
dc2tog	double crochet two stitches together
sc	single crochet
sk	skip
sp	space
st(s)	stitch(es)

gauge
13 sts to 4" over dc on
size I/9 (5.50 m) hook or
size needed to obtain
gauge

Body
Ch 49 (55, 61, 67)

ROW 1 Work 1 dc in third ch from hook and in next 6 (7, 8, 9) chs. In next ch work (2 dc, ch 2, 2 dc). Work 1 dc in next 7 (8, 9, 10) chs for sleeve. In next ch work (2 dc, ch 2, 2 dc). Work 1 dc in next 14 (16, 18, 20) chs for back. In next ch work (2 dc, ch 2, 2 dc). Work 1 dc in next 7 (8, 9, 10) chs for sleeve. In next ch work (2 dc, ch 2, 2 dc). Work 1 dc in next 8 (9, 10, 11) chs for front—59 (65, 71, 77) sts and 4 ch-2 sp.

ROW 2 Ch 2 and turn. Work 1 dc in each dc and (2 dc, ch 2, 2 dc) in each ch-2 sp—16 sts increased. You should have 75 (81, 87, 93) sts.

CHICK FEED
So far the sweaters in this book have all been flat-panel construction. This pattern is worked from the top down, all in one piece. This cardigan was inspired by an heirloom pattern but has been updated with a closer fit and a cute edging color.

ADVANCED BEGINNER

ROW 3   Repeat Row 2–91 (97, 103, 109) sts.

ROW 4   Repeat Row 2–107 (113, 119, 125) sts.

ROW 5   Ch 2 and turn. Work 1 dc in each dc and (1 dc, ch 1, 1 dc) in each ch-2 sp–8 sts increased. You should have 115 (121, 127, 133) sts.

ROW 6   Ch 2 and turn. Work 1 dc in each dc and (1 dc, ch 1, 1 dc) in each ch-1 sp–8 sts increased. You should have 123 (129, 135, 141) sts.

Repeat Row 6 another 8 (10, 12, 14) times. You should have 187 (209, 231, 253) sts.

DIVIDE FOR BODY AND SLEEVES

ROW 1   Ch 2 and turn. Work 1 dc in each of next 25 (28, 31, 34) sts for front, work 1 dc in ch-1 sp, sk next 43 (48, 53, 58) sts for sleeve, work 1 dc in ch-1 sp, 1 dc in each of next 50 (56, 62, 68) sts for back, work 1 dc in ch-1 sp, sk next 43 (48, 53, 58) sts for sleeve, work 1 dc in ch-1 sp, work 1 dc in each of next 26 (29, 32, 35) sts for other front.

ROW 2   Ch 2 and turn. Work 1 dc in each dc leaving sleeve sts for later–105 (117, 129, 141) sts.

Repeat Row 2 until panel measures 12″ from beg. Fasten off.

Sleeves

NOTE: SLEEVES ARE WORKED BACK AND FORTH, NOT AROUND AND AROUND.

Attach yarn at underarm. Evenly work 46 (51, 56, 61) sts around underarm.

ROW 1   Ch 2 and turn. Work 1 dc in each dc across.

ROW 2   Ch 2 and turn. Work 1 dc in each dc across.

ROW 3   Ch 2 and turn. Work 1 dc in each dc across.

ROW 4   Ch 2 and turn. Dc2tog over first 2 dc, work 1 dc in each dc across, dc2tog over last 2 dc–decrease 2 sts. You should have 44 (49, 54, 59) sts.

Repeat Rows 1-4 until sleeve measures 16″ from under the arm or to desired length.

Fasten off and repeat for other sleeve.

BUTTON BAND

Attach yarn at left front neck edge.

ROW 1   Work 1 sc in first st, *ch 1, 1 sc in next st*. Repeat from * to * down left front edge, ending with a sc in last st–38 (44, 50, 56) sc worked.

ROW 2   Ch 1 and turn. Sc in first sc and ch-1 sp, *ch 1, sk next sc, work 1 sc in ch-1 sp*. Repeat from * to * across ending with a sc in last sc.

Repeat Rows 1 and 2 2 more times. Fasten off.

BUTTONHOLE BAND

Attach yarn at right front bottom edge.

ROW 1   Work 1 sc in first st, *ch 1, 1 sc in next st*. Repeat from * to * down left front edge, ending with a sc in last st–38 (44, 50, 56) sc worked.

ROW 2   Ch 1 and turn. Sc in first sc and ch-1 sp, *ch 1, sk next sc, work 1 sc in ch-1 sp*. Repeat from * to * across, ending with a sc in last sc.

ROW 3   Buttonhole Row: Ch 1 and turn. Work 1 sc in first sc, *ch 3 and sk next (sc, ch-1 sp, sc). Work 1 sc in next ch-1 sp, (ch 1, sk next sc, work 1 sc in next ch-1 sp), 4 (5, 6, 7) times*. Repeat from * to * another 5 times. Ch 3 and sk next (sc, ch-1 sp, sc), work 1 sc in last sc– 7 buttonholes made.

ROW 4   Ch 1 and turn. Work 1 sc in first sc, in ch-3 sp work (sc, ch 1, sc). *Work (ch 1, 1 sc in next ch-1 sp) 4 (5, 6, 7) times and then ch 1. In ch-3 sp work (sc, ch 1, sc)*. Repeat from * to * another 5 times. Work 1 sc in last sc.

ROW 5   Ch 1 and turn. Work 1 sc in first st, *ch 1, 1 sc in next st*. Repeat from * to * across, ending with a sc in last st– 38 (44, 50, 56) sc worked.

ROW 6   Ch 1 and turn. Sc in first sc and ch-1 sp, *ch 1, sk next sc, work 1 sc in ch-1 sp*. Repeat from * to * across, ending with a sc in last sc.

Collar

ROW 1   Attach yarn at top right front edge. Work 8 sc evenly across right front edge, then 4 sc across shoulder edge, then 9 sc across back edge, 4 sc for other shoulder, and 8 sc for left front edge.

ROW 2   Ch 1 and turn. Work 1 sc in each sc across–33 sc.

Repeat Row 2 another 17 times. You should have 19 rows total. Fasten off and weave in all yarn ends.

Finishing

NOTE: BEFORE FINISHING: REFER TO LESSON 19, "GET IT TOGETHER," (PAGE 148) FOR INSTRUCTIONS ON VARIOUS FINISHING TECHNIQUES.

Using vertical mattress stitch, sew sleeve seams.

Sew buttons in place on button placket using buttonholes as a guide.

Weave in all yarn ends.

147

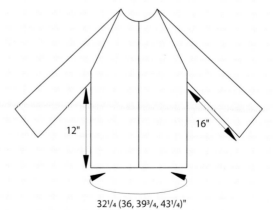

32¹/₄ (36, 39³/₄, 43¹/₄)"

Sewing & Finishing

Finishing is the grand finale of crochet. This art form that you have nurtured and devoted so much time to is finally taking shape. Learning to sew your garments together is a very important process of the whole crocheting experience and, as with all aspects of crocheting, it takes a little bit of time and practice but is definitely worth the effort. With a little pull here and a tug there, you'll be able to make your garment fit like a glove. Good finishing techniques can mean the difference between a runway-ready showpiece and a hopelessly homemade look.

148

Blocking

This process involves dampening or steaming your knitted pieces while they are shaped and smoothed by being pinned into place on an ironing board or other flat surface to dry. This reduces curling of the edges, making the pieces easier to sew together; it also will smooth out uneven stitches and can add inches to a knitted piece that was knit too small. However, some yarns today are purposely created to display the characteristics of uneven stitching. Also, some man-made fibers would loose their appearance and quality if blocked, so read your yarn labels carefully before undertaking this step.

WET BLOCKING

Wet the pieces either in a sink or in the washing machine, following yarn manufacter's instructions. Lay pieces down on a padded surface, such as folded towels on a carpet or bed, and gently pat them into place following desired measurements. Pin in place using rust-resistant pins and let garment dry.

STEAM BLOCKING

Pin down the edges of your pieces onto an ironing board so they are shaped and flat. If you need a little more room than an ironing board provides, you may use folded towels on a carpet or bed; blocking boards are even available for your convenience. Using a good steam iron, hold the iron over the pieces, making sure not to let it touch the fabric, and release the steam evenly. Smooth your crochet pieces flat and then let dry thoroughly.

Getting It All Together: Seaming

Seaming is a step that new crocheters tend to want to rush through. But don't! Take your time joining the pieces; you may have to try a seam several times before it looks perfect. Persevere; it will be the difference between homemade and handmade.

WHAT DO I USE TO SEW MY PROJECT TOGETHER?

Most often you will use the same yarn used to crochet your garment, but sometimes you will make a project with a yarn that just doesn't cooperate while seaming. It may be too bumpy or have fringy bits that make it difficult to pull through your crocheted piece. In that case, use a smooth yarn that is the same shade as your project. This will allow seaming to glide with little frustration. We do not recommend using thread, as it does not have the same stretch as yarn and could break too easily.

WHIPSTITCH SEAM

Whipstitch seams are very flat, so they may be a good choice when joining shoulder seams of a bulky project or joining squares together to make an afghan. Lay pieces flat with right sides facing up. Attach yarn and then insert needle from front

to back through back loops only of one piece of fabric, then from back to front through corresponding stitch of second piece of fabric in back loops only. Continue in this way along stitches, always starting on the same side of fabric. Fasten off and weave in all yarn ends.

SLIP STITCH SEAM

This is a very tight seam without a lot of give or stretch. We like to call this the "fix it" seam. Perhaps your foundation chain was too loose or the neckline edge of a sweater is a little too open. The slip stitch seam is your pal. It will tighten up those edges without adding extra length to the project, and it also gives a very firm seam for shoulder seams. Here's how it's done: Holding the pieces with right sides together, attach yarn to edge. *Insert hook in next pair of edge stitches, yarn over and draw loop through both stitches and the loop on the hook*. Repeat from * to * until all desired edge stitches have been worked. Fasten off and weave in all yarn ends.

SINGLE CROCHET SEAM

A single crochet seam has a little more give than a slip stitch seam. We like to use this seam when we want to highlight a seam or edge as an embellishment. With wrong sides together, attach yarn to edge. *Insert hook in next pair of edge stitches, yarn over and draw loop through both edge stitches. Yarn over and draw through two loops on hook*. Repeat from * to * until all desired edge stitches have been worked. Fasten off and weave in all yarn ends.

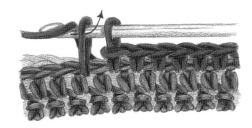

INVISIBLE MATTRESS SEAM

The Chicks' favorite seam for finishing leaves a clean, professional seam. The mattress seam is, as we said, invisible. When done correctly, it will be hard to tell where you joined pieces together. There are two types of invisible mattress seams: vertical and horizontal. When joining side seams, you'll use the vertical seam. When joining seams at the shoulders, you'll use the horizontal seam. How to make the seams is explained at right.

Vertical Mattress Stitch
(for vertical seaming)

This is a very good stitch to use for sewing together the sides of a garment. It allows for some stretch to the fabric while providing stability and a beautifully finished edge. Lay pieces flat with right sides facing up. Attach yarn at corner edge of one piece. *Insert needle vertically under and out of a stitch on one side then under and out of a stitch at the same spot on the other piece (1). Go back to the other side, moving up a row*. Repeat from * to * until all edge stitches have been worked (2). Pull gently on yarn to match tension to that of the garment. Fasten off and weave in all yarn ends.

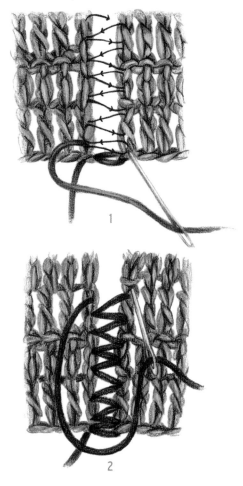

Horizontal Mattress Stitch
(for horizontal seaming)

This is a very good stitch to use for sewing together shoulders. Just like its vertical counterpart, it allows for some stretch to the fabric while providing stability and a beautifully finished edge. Lay pieces flat with right sides facing up. Attach yarn at corner edge of one piece. *Insert needle horizontally under and out of a stitch on one side then under and out of a stitch at the same stitch on the other piece (1). Go back to the other side, moving along to the next stitch*. Repeat from * to * until all edge stitches have been worked (2). Pull gently on yarn to match tension to that of the garment. Fasten off and weave in all yarn ends.

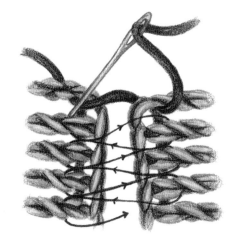

1

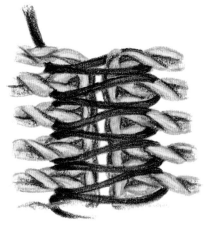

2

WELCOME TO THE CROCHET COMMUNITY

Crocheters, Unite!

Even if you only learned one stitch, you are now officially a crochet hooker! One of the most fabulous and rewarding parts of crochet is the community you can expose (well, we don't literally mean **expose**) yourself to. It doesn't matter if you live in a crowded city such as New York or a remote little town in North Dakota. You now have a common bond with thousand of others with the same interest.

Ways to Put More Crochet in Your Life

- Visit local yarn shops and craft stores
- Join the Crochet Guild of America (www.crochet.org)
- Join or form crochet clubs. Check your local library, bookstore, or church/synagogue for crochet or needlework group meetings.
- Join crochet chat rooms
- Peruse online crochet blogs
- Download crochet podcasts

The Benefits of Meeting Other Crocheters

- Having friends to share your passion for crochet
- Trading tips and techniques
- Learning new skills
- Teaching others the skills you know
- Sparking creativity
- Showing off your projects
- Swapping extra yarn
- Helping others by offering your skills for charity crocheting

Charity Crochet

Put your hands (and your newfound crochet skills) to work to make someone's life a little better. Trust us, nothing is more rewarding. There are hundreds of organizations looking for volunteers to crochet hats, blankets, and more for those in need. Try searching the Web for "crocheting for charity" and see what turns up or check with your local hospital, nursing home, or house of worship. Better yet, teach someone else to crochet along with you. You don't need a degree to teach others how to crochet. Senior centers, nursing homes, homeless shelters, and schools are often in need of crochet teachers. Remember the feeling of achievement and self-reliance you felt when you finished your first project? Share it with someone else!

Start Your Own Crochet Club

No clubs near you? Start your own! You only need one friend to get started, and your group can be as organized (or disorganized) as you like. Here are a few tips for setting up a successful crochet or needlework club.

- Set a regular time and place to meet.
- Post fliers where you want to reach other crocheters: library, community center, around your neighborhood, local yarn shops, church or synagogue, schools.
- Choose what you want to accomplish at a club meeting. You don't have to do anything more than sit and crochet, but if you want to get others interested, here are some of the fun things we suggest trying at a club meeting:

- Gear some meetings around teaching/learning a new skill, such as how to change colors, work in the round, or introduce more complex methods such as Tunisian crochet, filet crochet, etc.
- Plan a yarn swap: Have everyone bring in yarn he or she doesn't use, pile it up together on a table, and take turns picking out new yarn.
- Hold a potluck lunch or dinner at the meeting. Everyone brings a little something to contribute to the meal.
- Have a picnic rather than a meeting at your usual place.
- Have a raffle (give away yarn, needles, notions, books, etc.)
- Bring in guest speakers to cover particular topics: yarn care, finishing, garment construction, etc.
- Host a fashion show or a show-and-tell to show off the items you made.

FURTHER READING

There are a lot of great crochet books on the market. Many of them served as inspiration in our designs and stitch patterns and are must-haves for your crochet library:

The Complete Idiot's Guide to Knitting and Crocheting Illustrated, 3rd edition, by Barbara Breiter and Gal Diven (Alpha Books, 2006).

The Crochet Answer Book: *Solutions to Every Problem You'll Ever Face, Answers to Every Question You'll Ever Ask*, by Edie Eckman (Storey Publishing, 2007).

Crochet for Tots: *20 Fresh and Fun Designs*, by Nancy Queen (Martingale and Company, 2003).

The Encyclopedia of Crochet Techniques: *A Step-by-Step Guide to Creating Unique Fashions and Accessories*, by Jan Eaton (Running Press Book Publishers, 2006).

RESOURCES

Crochet Clubs & Associations

Crochet Guild of America (www.crochet.org)

Crochet Websites

www.thechickswithsticks.com

www.crochetme.com

ACKNOWLEDGMENTS

Heather Walpole: Thanks for designing and making the samples for three awesome projects: Felted Zebra Slippers, Heather's Café Cardigan, Surfer Chick Quick Cap

Joy Aquilino & Amy Vinchesi, our editors: Thanks for keeping us on our toes.

And a VERY special thanks to our customers for their daily encouragement, support, and—most of all—enthusiasm!

154

Nancy Queen

Hometown: The perfectly preppy Wayne, PA

Favorite Color: Lime green, but if zebra stripes were a color, they would win.

Favorite Food: Popcorn

Zodiac Sign: Aries

Family Life: Makes a happy home with husband, Ben; daughter, Hadley; and pampered Maltese pooch, Angel

Favorite Movie: 80s flicks like **Trading Places**, **Sixteen Candles**, **Secret of my Success**, and **Better Off Dead**

Favorite Music for Crocheting: Van Morrison, Coldplay

Favorite Spot to Crochet: In bed, watching TV with my husband, dog, and daughter

How Mary Ellen Describes Nancy: "She gets an idea in her head and, Look out, Momma, comin' through!"

Favorite Project: Small stuff such as hats, stuffed animals, vests, mittens, and kids' clothes.

Favorite Fiber: Alpaca

Something Most People Don't Know About Her: She occasionally falls asleep with crochet hook in hand.

Favorite Part of a Project: Getting started

Least Favorite Part of a Project: Finishing it!

Motto: So much yarn, so little time.

Favorite Thing to Do When Not Crocheting: Shopping. Turns into a Chick with a credit card, and knows how to use it.

Mary Ellen O'Connell, a.k.a. Meo

Hometown: Time split between Malvern, PA, and Naples, FL

Favorite Color: Bling!

Favorite Food: Peanut M&M's

Zodiac Sign: Virgo

Family life: Long-time marriage to doting husband, Chris. Two grown boys, Dan and Dave, who are out of the house

Favorite Movie: The **Indiana Jones** series (guess that's where the adventuresome spirit comes from)

Favorite Music for Crochet: Country, especially Trace Atkins, Pat Green, and Toby Keith

Favorite Spot to Crochet: Poolside

How Nancy Describes Mary Ellen: "She's the Texas-Florida-Philly girl with the Boston accent."

Favorite Project: The one I'm working on at the time.

Favorite Fiber: Ditto

Motto: I'll try anything (okay, almost anything) once.

Favorite Part of a Project: Selecting the yarn

Least Favorite Part of a Project: Picking up stitches.

Something Most People Don't Know About Her: She can't start the day without a cup of coffee and working a few rows on her current project in progress.

Favorite Thing to Do When Not Crocheting She's still a Chick with a stick: When she's not holding her crochet hook or knitting needles, she's out on the green with golf club securely in hand.

- Need something to wear to a party this weekend? Chicks love fast, easy accessories that can be worked in as little as a few hours. Cinderella's goin' to the ball! Bibbidi-bobbidi-boo!
- Need to keep your hands busy? Chicks love a project that can be worked mindlessly while zoning in front of the tube, waiting in the carpool lane, or sitting in the doctor's office. Crochet, take me away!
- Sick of scarves? Chicks love projects that take crocheting to the next level—without complicating the issue. Simple shells, trendy shrugs, and funky felted handbags—everything a fashion-forward girl can't live without!
- Feeling frazzled? Chicks combat stress by stitching. Just get going and crochet your problems away!
- Just do it! Chicks love a crocheter who dives right in. Technique comes with practice; until then just enjoy the ride.
- Be a crochet diva. Chicks love all the beaded stitch markers, beautiful bags, leopard-spotted hooks, and other gorgeous tools that have been popping up all over. Add a few to your supply list and look great while you stitch.

HOROSCOPES

What kind of crocheter are you? Consult the stars to find out!

ARIES (March 21-April 19): You are a rambunctious ram who likes to keep busy even when plunked in front of the TV. Find projects that will keep your creative juices flowing. Interesting stitches and novelty yarns will keep even the most spirited ram from getting bored!

TAURUS (April 20-May 20): Your warmhearted and lovable nature means you adore making gifts for others. You'll love all the newfound projects you'll be able to make for others now that you crochet!

GEMINI (May 21-June 20): Your adaptability and versatility will make you a quick study in the art of crochet. Your witty personality and good communication skills make you a natural teacher. Contact your local yarn shop; they could use your help.

CANCER (June 21-July 22): You are imaginative and loving. Start a crochet club in your community. Since you are always willing to lend a sympathetic ear, others will be flocking to join your group!

LEO (July 23-August 22): Let your enthusiastic creativity abound in crochet. Your broad-mindedness will open unlimited possibilities to this art for you.

VIRGO (August 23-September 22): Your perfectionist nature means you'll keep practicing your crochet, Virgo, until you've mastered every technique! Having the most perfect stitches isn't everything though—just remember to have a little fun. After all, this is a hobby!

LIBRA (September 23-October 22): Always the peacemaker, you are destined to join a crochet club. With your easygoing and sociable nature, you'll be the glue that holds it all together.

SCORPIO (October 23-November 21): Your determination will keep you crocheting, Scorpio. Once you've mastered the skill, your passion for the craft will inspire others to join you.

SAGITTARIUS (November 22-December 21): You like to get right to the point, which makes our straightforward method just the ideal way for you to learn. Grab that hook and get started—you'll love the sense of freedom and satisfaction you get from crocheting a project.

CAPRICORN (December 22 - January 19): Don't let your cautious streak keep you from trying something new. Any mistake is easily fixed in crochet, so use your patience, perseverance, and sense of humor to stick with it.

AQUARIUS (January 20-February 18): Your independent nature makes you a natural self-starter. Pick up your hook and yarn (and this book) and start stitching. Always original, you'll be sure to create something cool!

PISCES (February 19 - March 20): Draw on your humanitarian and inventive sides and organize a crochet-for-charity event. You always feel great when you help others, so it's just like you to find something you love to do and put it to good use.

INDEX

159